BrainStrains®

D0673075

Eye•Popping
Puzzles

BrainStrains®

Eye○Popping
Puzzles

Frank Coussement
Peter De Schepper
Keith Kay

Sterling Publishing Co., Inc.

New York

Library of Congress Cataloging-in-Publication Data Available

10 9 8 7 6 5

Published by Sterling Publishing Co., Inc.
387 Park Avenue South, New York, NY 10016
© 2004 by Sterling Publishing Co., Inc.
Distributed in Canada by Sterling Publishing
c/o Canadian Manda Group, 165 Dufferin Street,
Toronto, Ontario, Canada M6K 3H6
Distributed in Great Britain by Chrysalis Books Group PLC
The Chrysalis Building, Bramley Road, London W10 6SP, England
Distributed in Australia by Capricorn Link (Australia) Pty. Ltd.
P.O. Box 704, Windsor, NSW 2756, Australia

Printed in China
All rights reserved

ISBN 1-4027-0990-0

For information about custom editions, special sales, premium and
corporate purchases, please contact Sterling Special Sales
Department at 800-805-5489 or specialsales@sterlingpub.com

Table of Contents

Introduction

BrainStrains® Eye-Popping Puzzles will challenge your mind and provide hours of fun and mental stimulation. Visual and number puzzles — and mind-blowing colorful optical illusions — will test, tone, and sharpen your thinking skills.

Note: Tips are provided for a good many of the BrainSnack puzzles and can be found starting on page 284. Refer to them, or not, as you wish. Solutions to all, as usual, are located at the back of the book.

BrainSnack®

Puzzles

A What cake (1–4) does not belong in this row?

Tip

B To economize on costs, a baker has progressively diminished the number of chocolate lines on his cakes. How many lines will there be on the next cake?

Tip

We have here three groups of mushrooms with only
the front face visible. The back side of each mushroom has
one dot less than the front side. How many
white dots are missing on the front side
of the last mushroom?

Tip

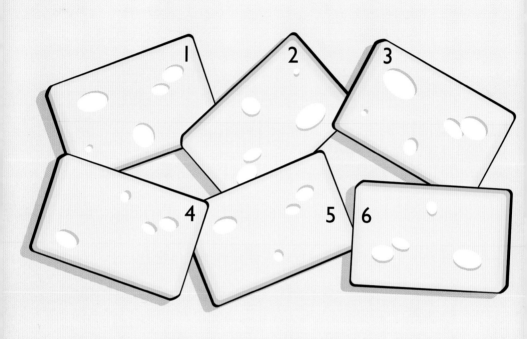

Only five out of these six slices of cheese have been cut from the same cheese block. Which slice (1–6) has been cut from a different cheese block?

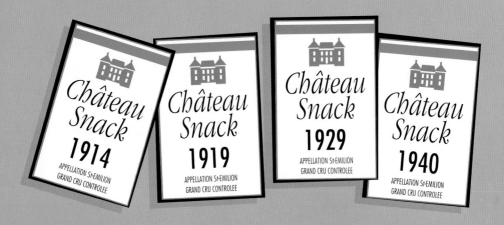

A connoisseur in wine, who only drinks "Château Snack,"
buys a series of bottles. It would appear, though, that
the dates of vintage follow a strange logic.
What will be the vintage year to appear on
the label of the next bottle?

Tip

Brian has divided the letters over four soup bowls and is now looking for a word. The first letter only appears in the fourth bowl. The second letter appears six times in all. The third letter appears twice in two bowls. The fourth letter appears once in the second bowl and once in the third bowl, but does not appear in the fourth bowl. The last letter appears once in the first bowl and twice in another bowl. What word is he looking for?

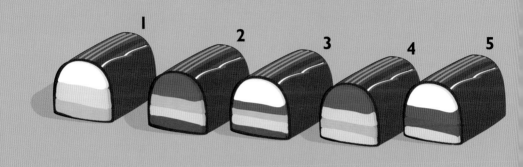

Brian is particularly fond of those famous Belgian chocolates called "pralines," but not just any variety. He loves the pralines that have brown, white, and red filling. He doesn't care for yellow or pink filling. Then again, he enjoys pralines with yellow and white filling, or pink and brown filling. Which of the above pralines will Brian choose?

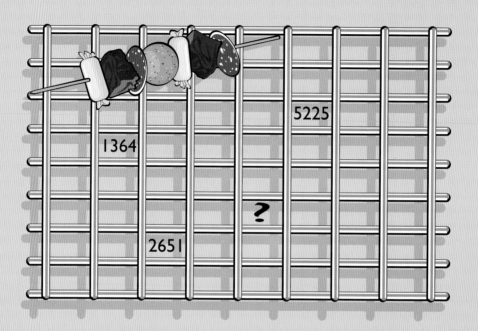

Which number on the grill has been replaced by
a question mark?

Tip

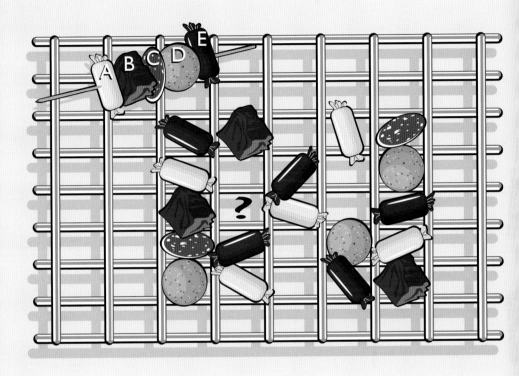

Five pieces each of five different kinds of meat were cooked on the 5 by 5 section of grill above. Considering the fact that, when the grill section was completely filled in, no two identical pieces of meat were positioned next to each other on either the horizontal or vertical axis, which piece of meat (A–E) was taken from the question mark position.

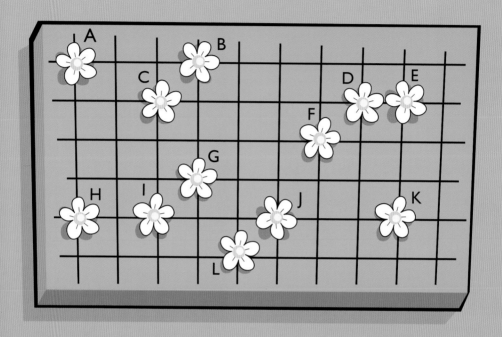

Walk from flower A to flower F following the grid lines, and pick all the flowers without using the same line or intersection twice. What is the minimum number of intersections you will have to pass through (not counting the starting intersection)?

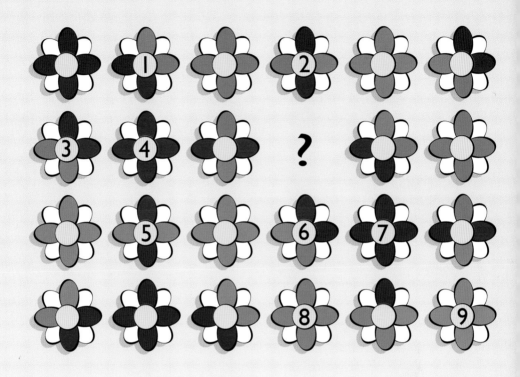

Which flower (1–9) has been replaced by the question mark?

Tip

Which ball (1–5) differs from the other four?

Tip

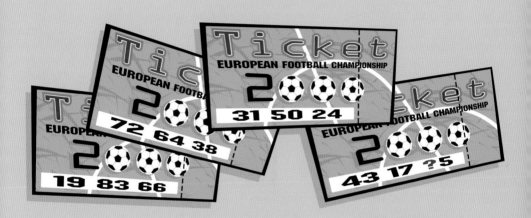

These tickets have been numbered following a special kind of logic. Which number is missing from the last ticket?

Tip

As a championship proceeds, more and more yellow cards are being distributed. On the first day, there were 17 of them, and on the fourth day, 35. Discover the logical link that exists between the numbers and you will know the number of yellow cards that will be drawn on the fifth day.

Tip

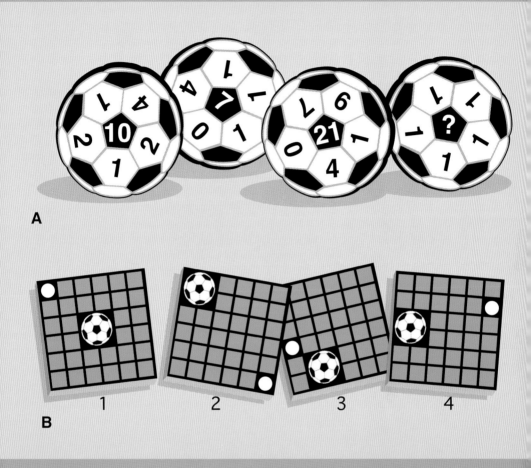

A. Which number is missing in the center of
the last ball?

Tip

B Selecting any one of three of the above tiles will allow you
to lay a floor that shows a particular repeating pattern.
Which tile cannot be used to lay a floor with that pattern?

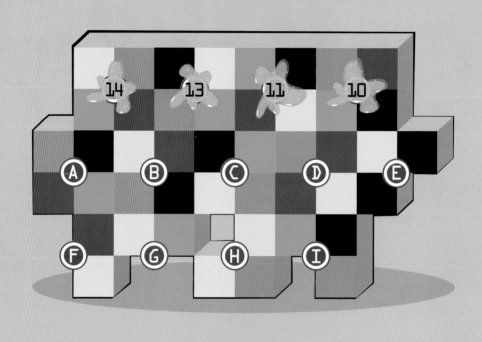

On top of this paintball wall, you can see how much certain color combinations are worth. Each of the five colors has a different value, ranging from 1 to five points. Where (A–I) can you earn 12 poiints?

Tip

How many logos, such as the one above left, can you
make with the other rings?

Tip

Which is the "real" gun among the
starter's pistols.

Tip

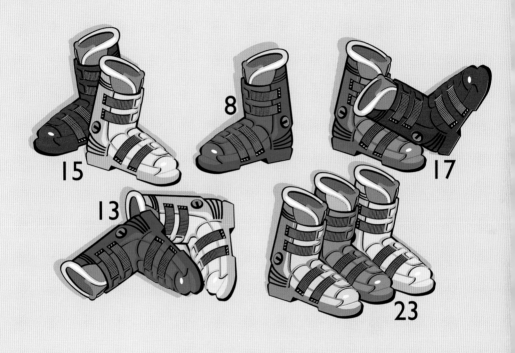

Based on the prices of the sets shown above,
how much does a gray ski boot cost?

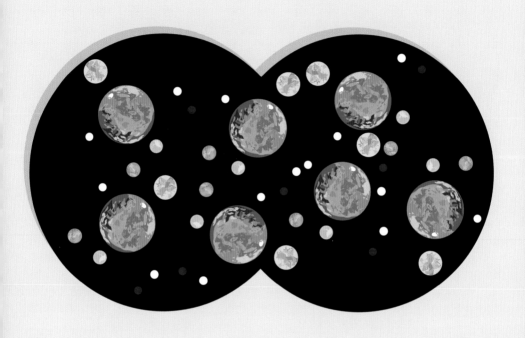

From the time exposure above, how many moons
are orbiting the blue planet?

Tip

Which liquid (1–8) has the highest specific gravity?

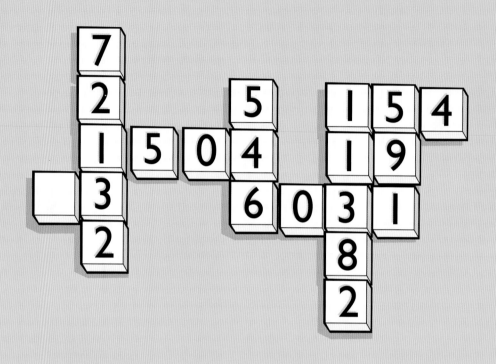

Which number is missing on the blank square?

Tip

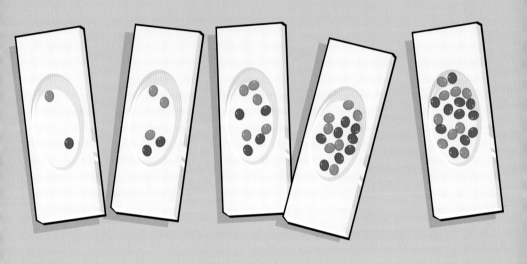

How many microbes are missing on the last test plate?

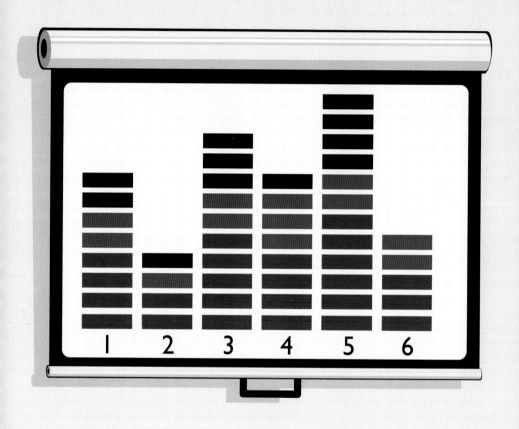

How many cubes are missing on the sixth stack?

Tip

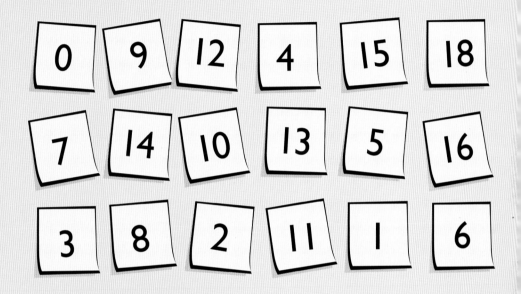

Which two pages must be swapped in order to
adhere to a certain logic?

Tip

Indicate the code of the combination lock that does not belong to this series.

Tip

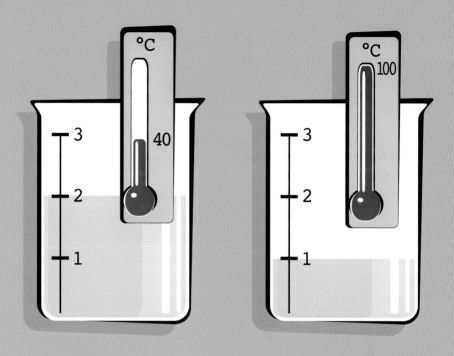

Having mixed 2 liters of water at a temperature off 40°C with 1 liter of water at a temperature of 100°C, what will be the temperature of the resulting mixture (excluding any heat losses)? You may use parentheses and rearrange the numbers any way you like.

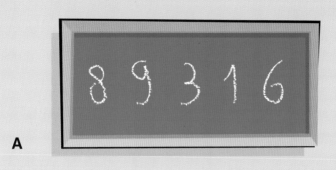

A

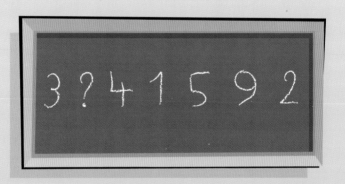

B

A Which is the largest number you can obtain by doing the standard calculations (addition, subtraction, multiplication, division) with these figures? You must do all four operations and can use each figure only once.

Tip

B Which number has been replaced by a question mark?

Tip

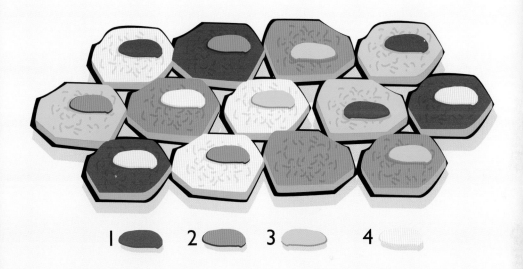

Which cell nucleus (1–4) belongs with the cell
that doesn't have a nucleus?

Tip

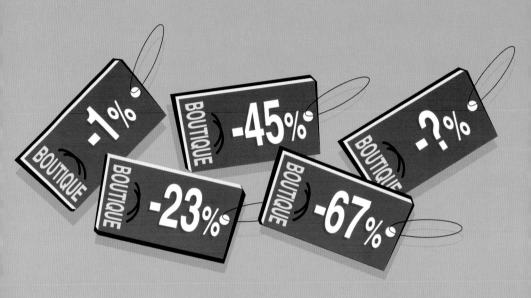

Discounts in this shop are increased as the sales period
nears the end. What will be the discount percentage
on the last price tag?

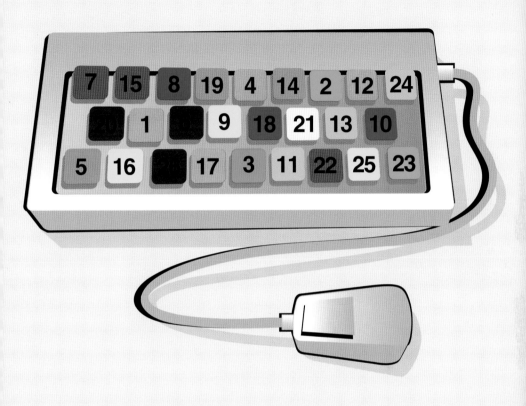

What should be the color of key 21? Answer with the number of a key that has the right color.

Tip

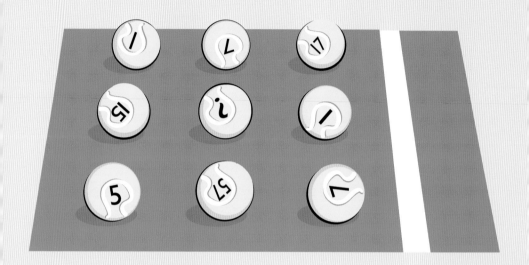

Which number is missing on the tennis ball that has the question mark?

What we have here is a dissected shape. The faces have been decorated with a triangular pattern. In which sector (A–F) of the upper face is the triangular motive missing?

Tip

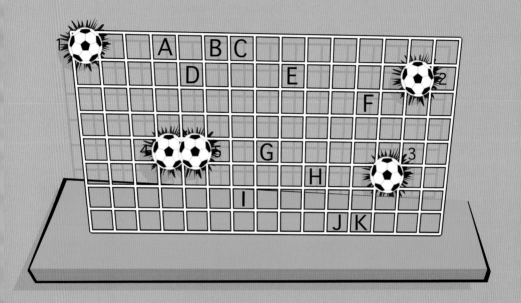

Five goals have been scored during the match, in a certain logical sequence. Where (A–K) will the ball for the sixth goal end up?

Tip

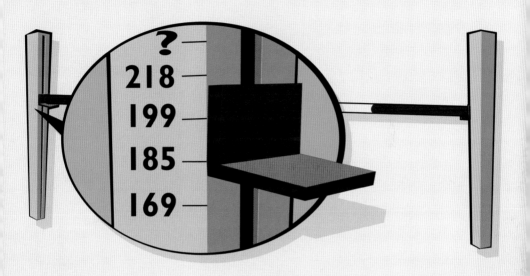

How high will the athlete jump next time?

Tip

A

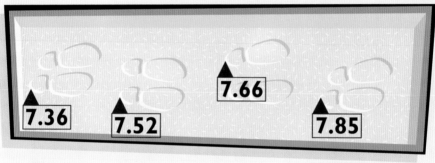

B

A The archer is shooting at the target by following a certain logic. How many arrows will he have put into the circles of the last target?

Tip

B How far will this athlete jump on his next try?

Tip

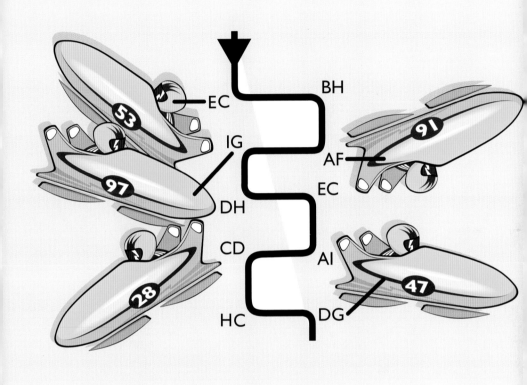

At what point (EC–DG) will bobsled number 28 leave the track?

Tip

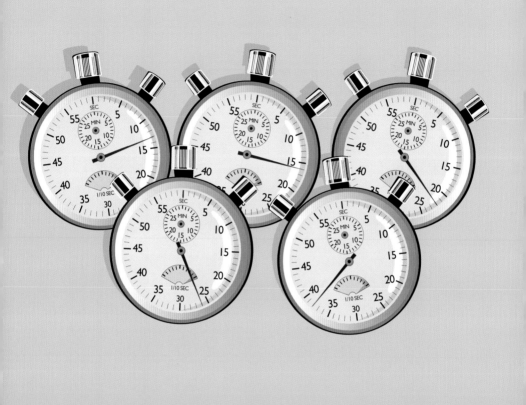

The winner has run the distance in 13 seconds, the runner-up in 16 seconds, etc. How many seconds will it take the sixth athlete to cross the line?

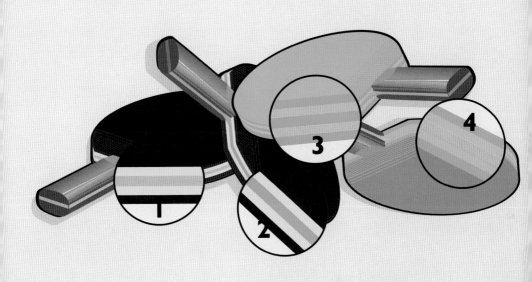

Three of the four table tennis paddles have been made by the same manufacturer. Bearing in mind that this manufacturer has only four different colors to work with, which paddle did he decide not to make?

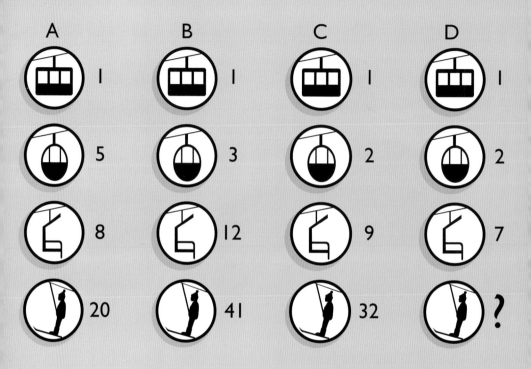

How many tow lifts must be added to ski area D?

Tip

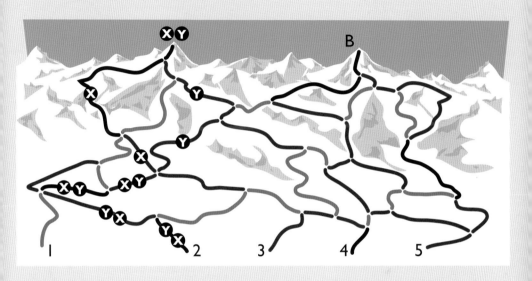

If the skier follows tracks X and Y, he will end up at point 2. Where will he arrive (1–5) if he leaves point B and follows a similar trail?

Tip

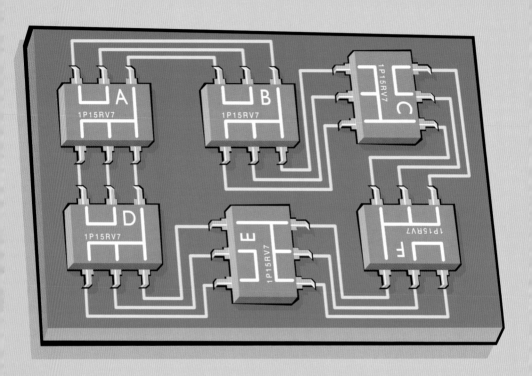

Which computer chip (A–F) has been incorrectly welded
on the circuit board?

Tip

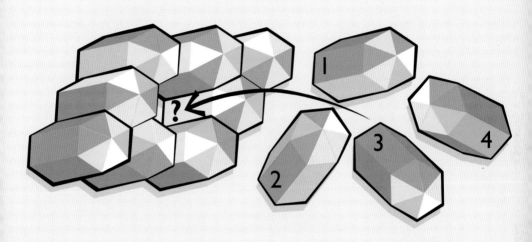

Which crystal (1–4) fits in the center of
the big crystal structure?

Tip

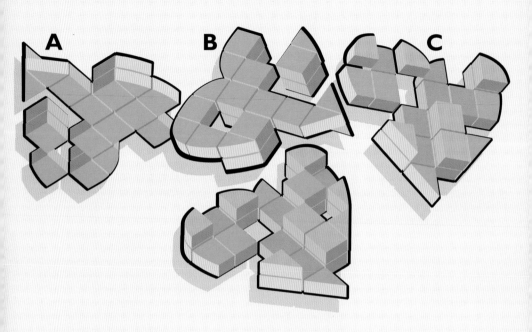

Which section of the heart (A–C) fits on the bottom piece?

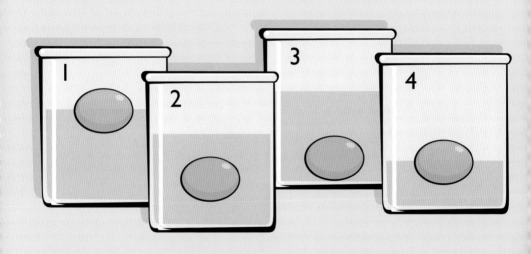

Here you have four measuring glasses containing a saline liquid and an egg. In which glass will you find the highest level of salt?

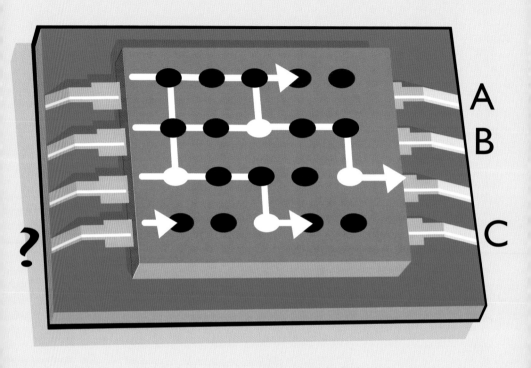

If you start at the question mark, where (A–C) will
the print line of the chip end up?

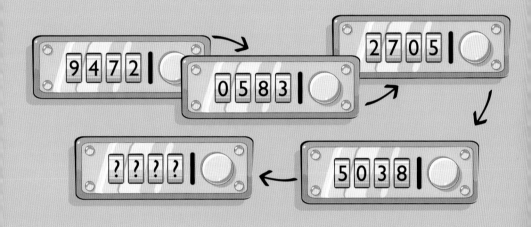

The secret code on this combination lock is changed regularly. What will the next secret code look like?

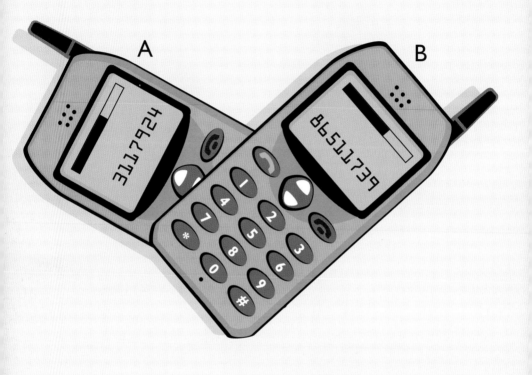

The mobile phone suffers from a design error. In phone A, the number 195702 has been punched but the number that is being displayed is 3117924. What telephone number has been punched in phone B?

Tip

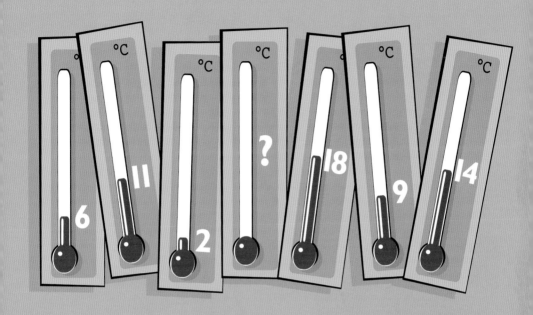

What temperature is missing on the thermometer
in the middle?

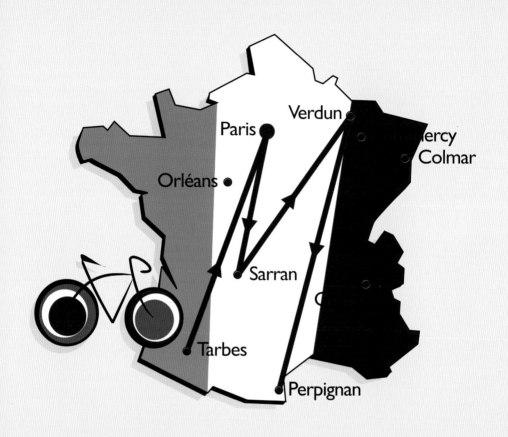

The riders start in Tarbes. In which city will the finishing line be found?

Tip

What is the number of the rider who will fall at
road bend number 7?

Tip

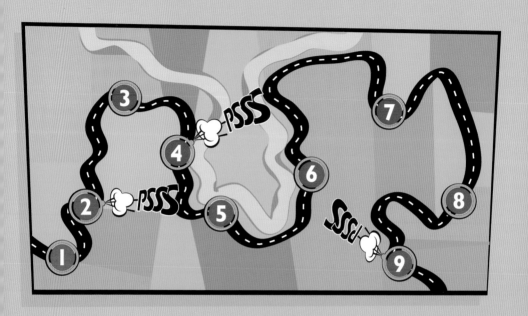

This rider has had a puncture four times during this 247.9 km-long ride. Indicate the number of the place where a puncture is missing.

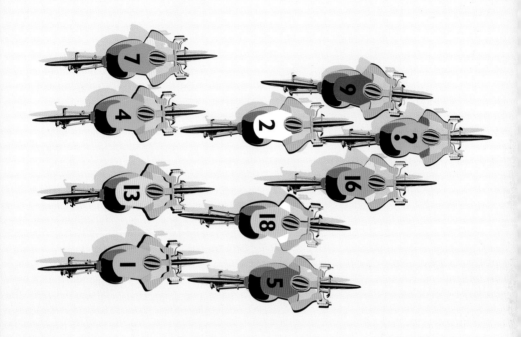

Which number is missing on the jersey of the
first rider?

Tip

At what other number do the riders get a drink?

Find out which numbers have been replaced by the
question marks and then indicate the total cost
of the cycling equipment.

Tip

Each square of a particular color replaces a particular number. Do the addition. Which number has been replaced by a question mark?

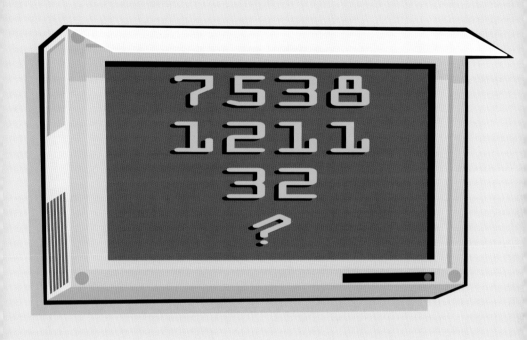

Which number has been replaced by
a question mark?

Tip

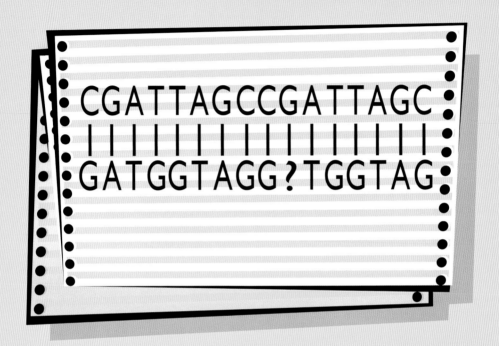

Which protein (A, T, C, or G) on this DNA string has
been replaced by a question mark?

Tip

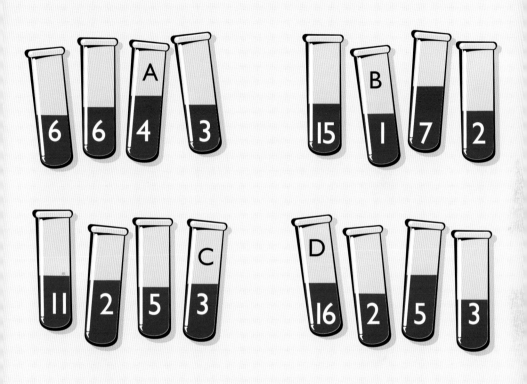

These are blood samples taken from four different patients. In which blood sample (A–D) is the count of red blood cells wrong?

Tip

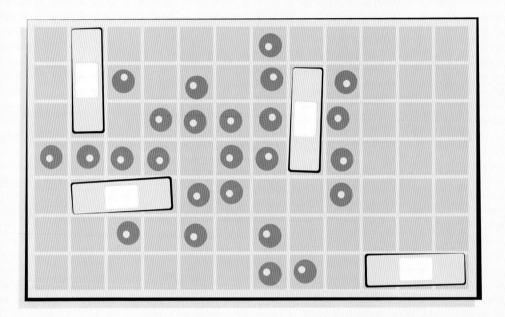

Indicate the minimum number of bandages needed to cover all of the wounds, considering the fact that each covers a maximum of three wounds on a horizontal or vertical axis and bearing in mind that the bandages are allowed to overlap.

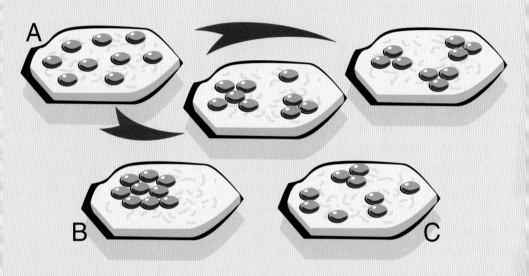

When cell A is submitted to genetic manipulation, the cell parts cluster together following a certain logic. Two different results of such manipulations are shown. Which situation (B or C), could be the result of another manipulation of cell A?

Tip

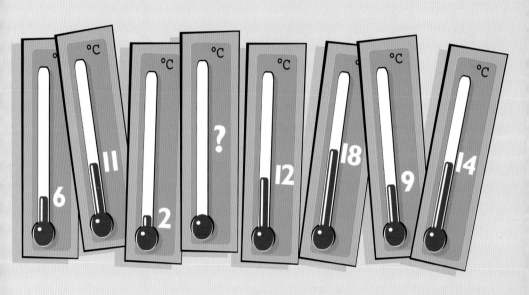

Which temperature indication is missing on
the fourth thermometer?

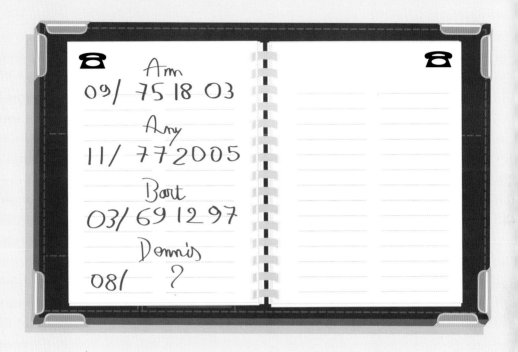

What telephone number is missing
in this Londoner's notebook?

Tip

A

C

E

B

D

Which ball (A–E) is different from the others?

Tip

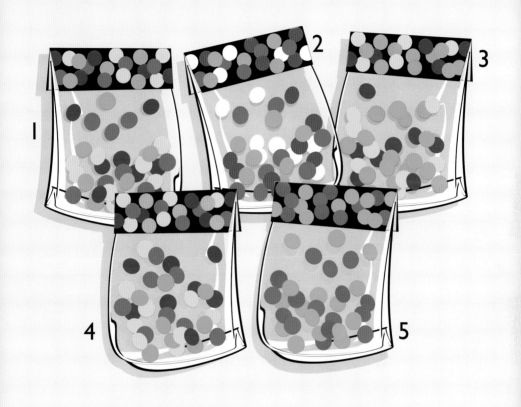

A mistake has been made on one of these bags
of confetti. Which bag (1–5)?

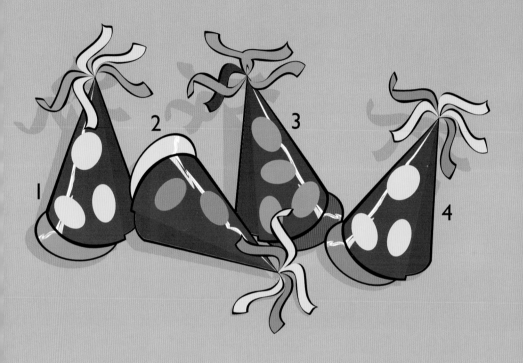

Which party hat (1–4) does not fit into this collection?

Tip

A What word are we looking for?

Tip

B The weights of four bells and their clappers are shown above. How much does the clapper of the last bell weigh?

Tip

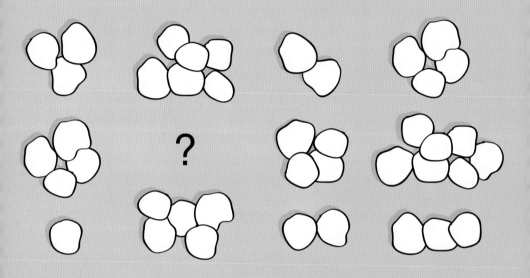

How many snowballs are hidden by the
question mark?

Tip

How many windows must be opened on the top floor?

Which word is hidden four times in the confetti?

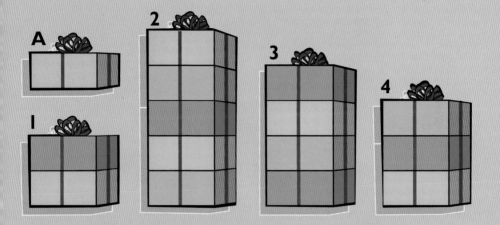

On which stack (1–4) does package A belong?

?
1665
1515
1385
1265

The snow has been thawing for four days. At what altitude will the thaw line be set at on the fifth day?

Tip

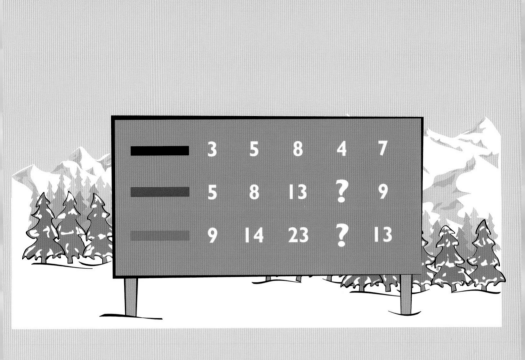

On the board, a distance indication is missing on the red and blue tracks. What should each one read?

Tip

What figure has been replaced by
a question mark?

Tip

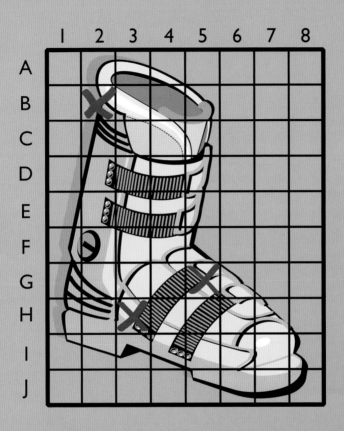

The crosses indicate three of the four places where the ski boot pinches. What are the coordinates?

Tip

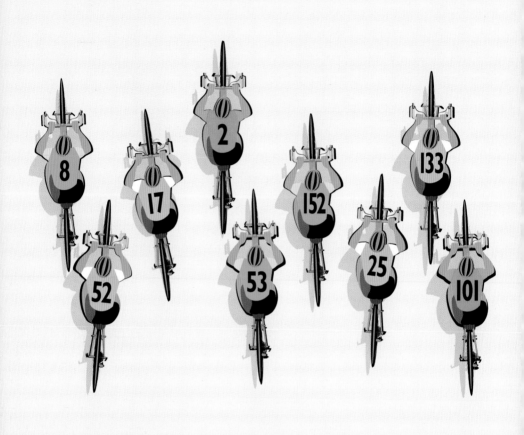

Which rider's number is wrong?

Tip

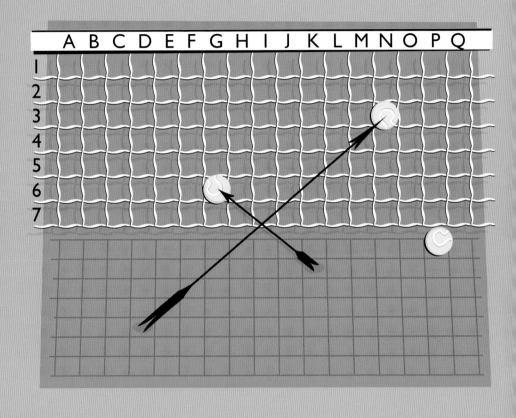

Indicate the coordinates of the spot where the third
tennis ball will hit the net.

Tip

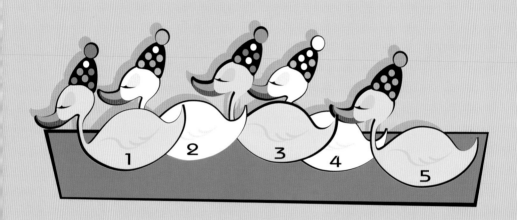

Which duck does not belong in the row?

Tip

The painting on the beach cabins (1–4) follows the pattern on cabins A and B. On which cabin did the painter go wrong?

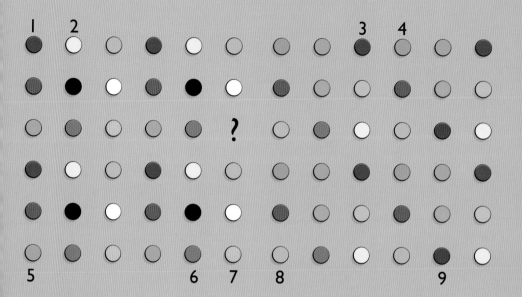

Which confetti (1–9) has been replaced by the question mark?

Tip

Which beach ball (1–5) does not belong to the set?

Tip

Which champagne glass (1–5) on the bottom row will be filled first, if you start filling the glasses from the top?

How many red stars will there be on the last rocket?

Tip

At least how many bags of type 3 have been showered, given the fact that two type 1 bags and one type 2 bag have been thrown and that each bag contains only one piece of black confetti?

Tip

Carnival hat number 1 is worn by the Prince, the highest in rank. The other hats are worn by subjects of the Prince in a decreasing ranking order. What will be the ranking order of hat A, bearing in mind that hat 3 is ranking fourth?

Tip

Each candy egg is seen here in its wrapped form and unwrapped and cut in half. There are eggs in white chocolate, milk chocolate, and dark chocolate. Which egg (1–7) has been wrongly wrapped?

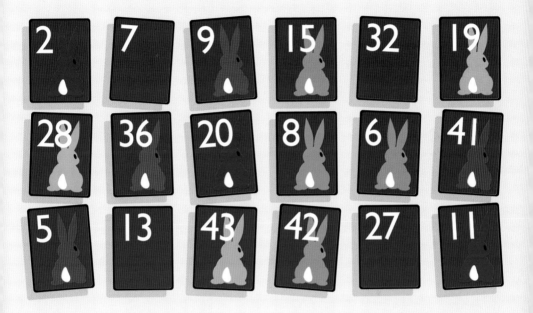

A number of Easter rabbits are missing, but it should be possible to calculate the number of differently colored rabbits. How many different colors will have been used once all the rabbits are made visible?

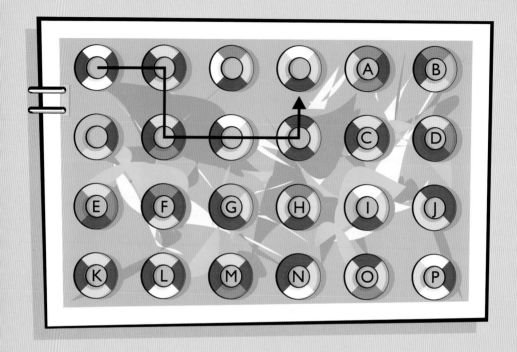

Which water ring (A–P) will the swimmer reach if he
pursues the logical orientation of the arrow as
long as possible?

Tip

This surf race has been won by surfer number 7648912 and surfer number 8637331 came in third. What is the number on the sail of the surfer that came in second?

Tip

Which protection factor is missing on the suntan oil
with the question mark?

Tip

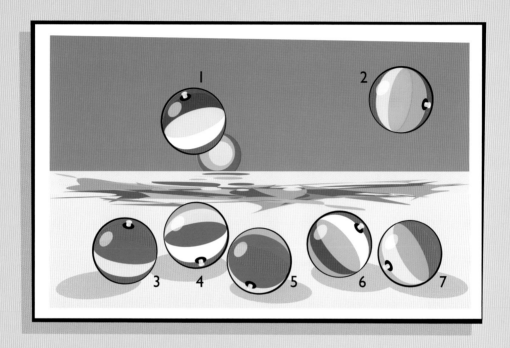

Which beach ball does (1–7) does not fit in
with this set?

Tip

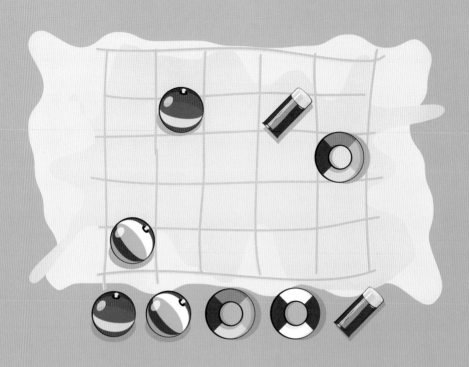

Fill this grid with all of the five objects in such a way that each object occurs on each horizontal, vertical, and diagonal axis only once.

You see here half of a beach ball with bands in six different colors. How many blue bands will there be on the invisible side of the ball?

Tip

A What is the time on the fifth digital clock?

Tip

B Which of these six digital clocks does not fit here?

Tip

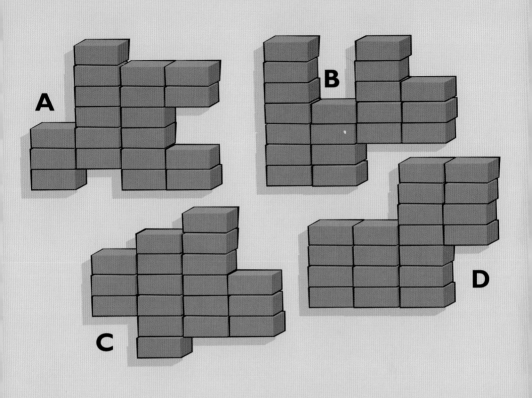

Which figure (A–D) does not belong here?

Tip

Brian wanted to send his friend a self-printed greeting card. However, he made a printing error. What did Brian actually want to write?

Five of these six pieces of colored glass suffice to make a perfectly square stained-glass window. Which is the piece you will not be needing to make this window?

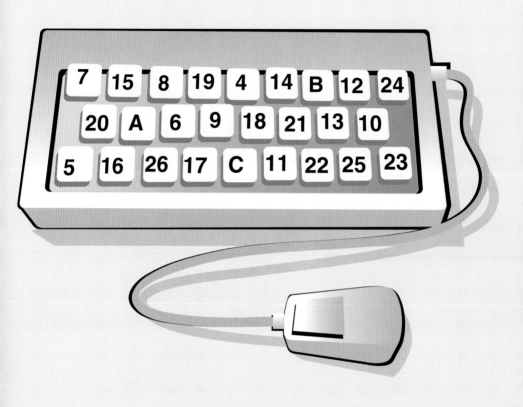

An industrial designer has developed a new keyboard.
He shows you three letters. Give the number of the key that
will be allocated to the letter Q.

Tip

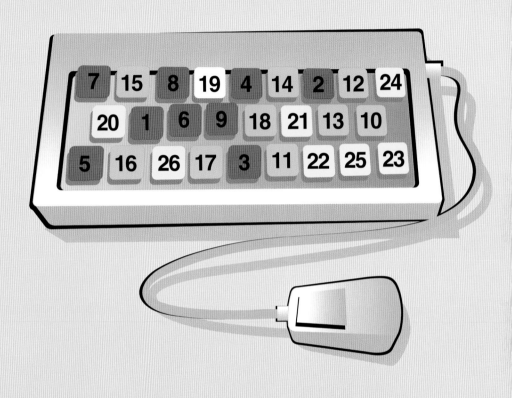

Each key has been given a certain color except for key 19. What will be the color for key 19?

Tip

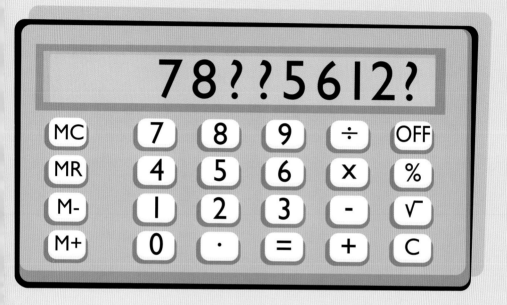

Which numbers are missing on the screen?

Tip

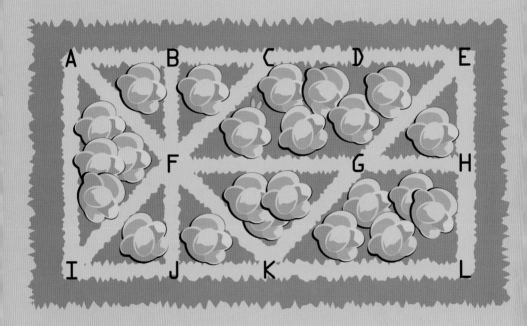

It's impossible to see through the trees and the shrubs in this wood. What is the minimum number of hunters it takes to guard all the paths and where (A–L) should those guards be placed?

Tip

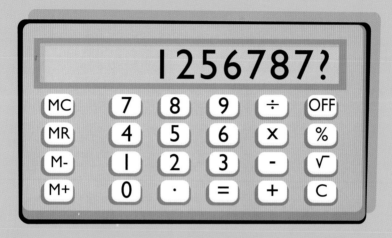

There is a problem with this calculator. The following figures have been successively introduced: 123596473489742, but a different figure is displayed on the screen. Which is the figure that has been replaced by the question mark?

Tip

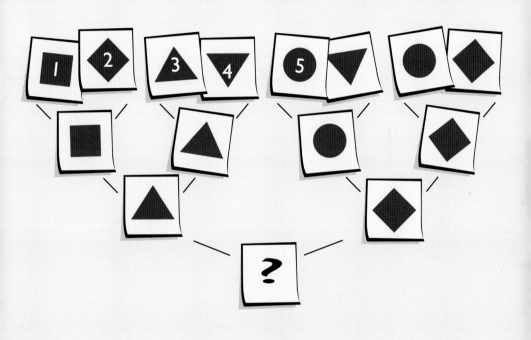

Which shape (1–5) will eventually win out?

Which figure needs to be erased in order to respect the underlying logic of the series of figures?

Tip

Which number has been replaced by the question mark?

Tip

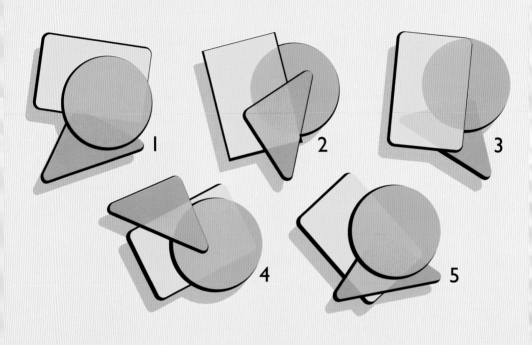

Which stack (1–5) of colored glass does not
belong here?

Tip

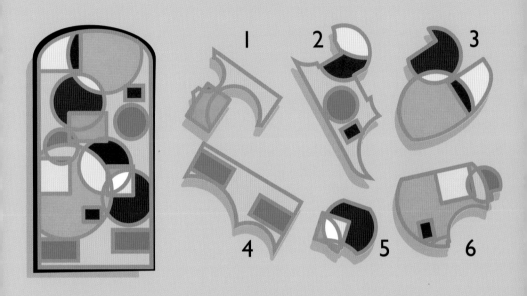

The stained glass window has been broken in six pieces.
Which piece (1–6) is seen in reverse?

Put the numbered license plates in a logical order,
starting with plate number 3.

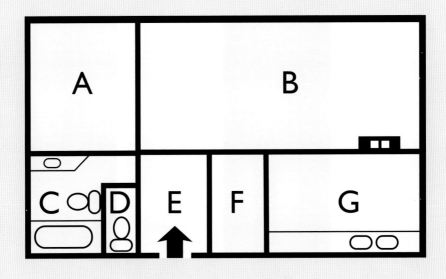

To enter this apartment, just follow the arrow.
At a minimum, how many doors will you have to go
through to make each room (A–G) accessible?

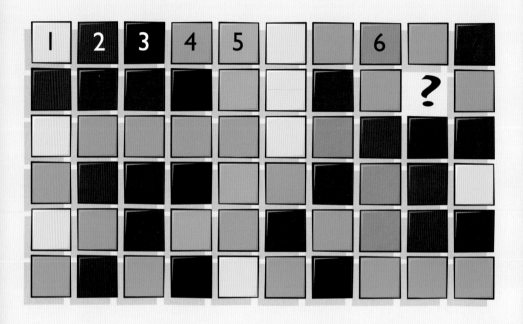

Which square (1–7) has been replaced by the
question mark?

On which parking space (1–7) is a black car missing?

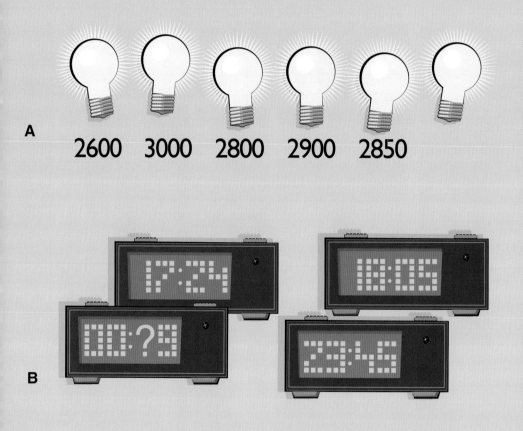

A

2600 3000 2800 2900 2850

B

A For how many hours will the last bulb burn?

Tip

B On the digital clock, which number has been
replaced by the question mark?

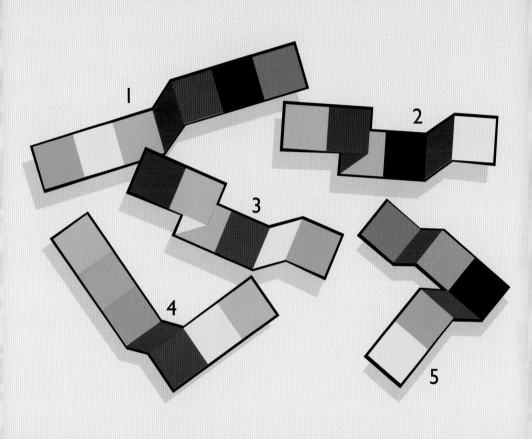

Which strip of colored paper (1–5) has not been folded correctly?

Tip

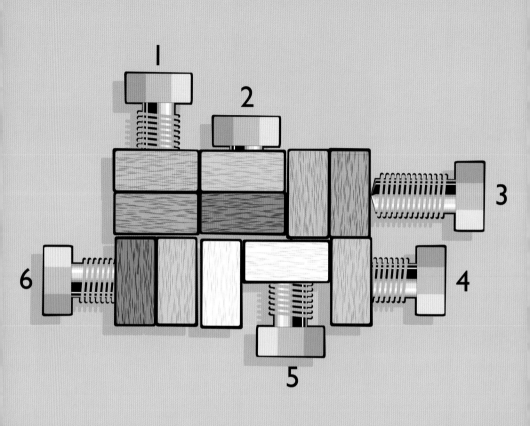

In a number of blocks, a screw thread has been cut into the holes. Other blocks do not have threaded holes. Which situation (1–6) presented is wrong, given that all the blocks of the same color are identical and that all the screws are equally long.

Tip

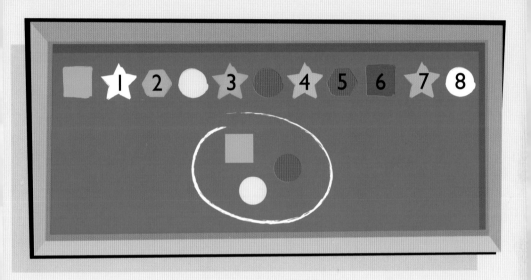

One form is missing in this set. Which form (1–8)
are we looking for?

Tip

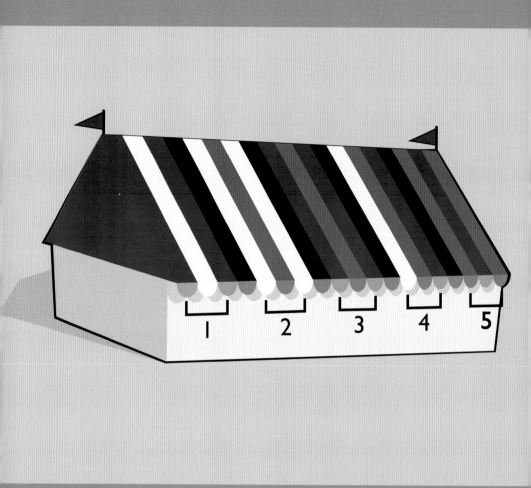

Which strip (1–5) of this canvas, consisting of three colored bands separated each time by a black band, has been given the wrong color?

Tip

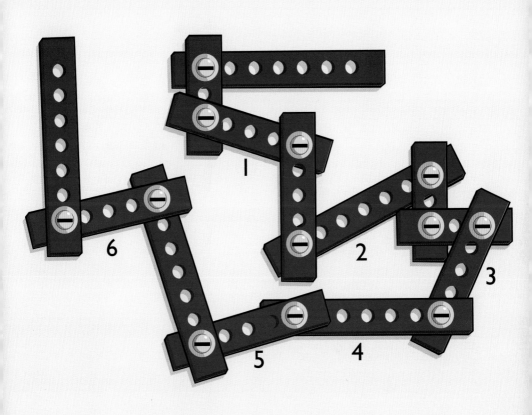

Which strip (1–6) is in the wrong place?

Tip

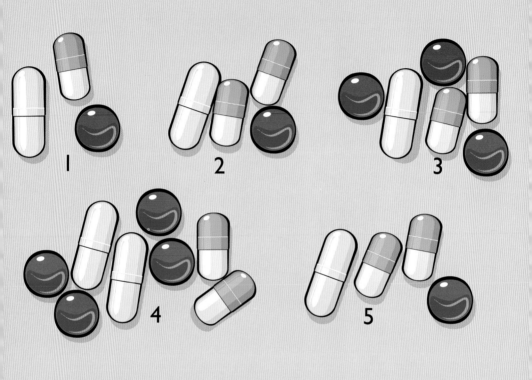

A doctor told a patient to take 25 pills over a period of six days. To get well as soon as possible, he was to take a different combination of pills each time. How many round pills will the patient have taken on the sixth day?

Tip

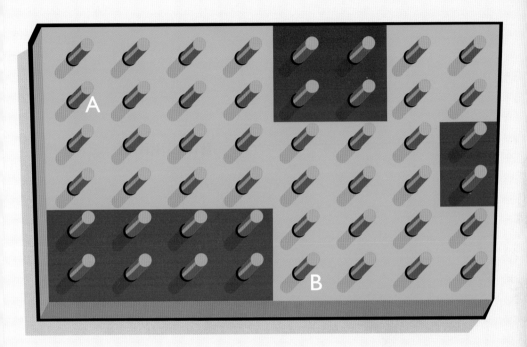

Go from A to B by linking as many rods as possible in the green area. The links may only be horizontal and vertical and a rod can only be used once. You may not move onto the red areas. How many units (a unit being the space between two rods) can you use?

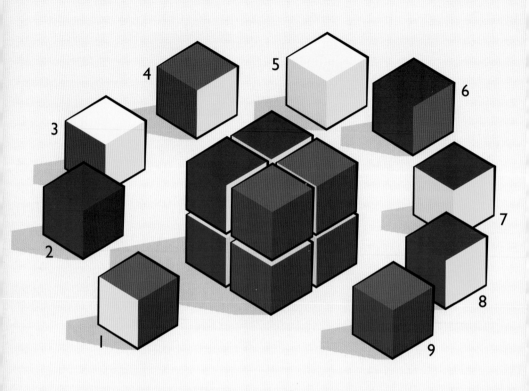

Here you have 9 blocks. You need 8 of them to build the cube in the middle. The cube has only two color halves and the contact faces of the blocks all have the same color everywhere. Each block has two colors. Which block (1–9) cannot be used?

Tip

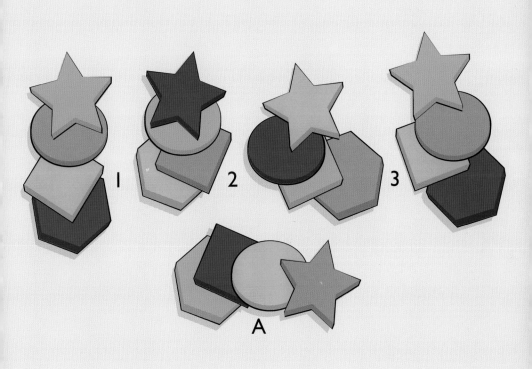

Where (1–3) should you put pile A?

Which two stained glass windows must change places in order to reveal the logic of the artist?

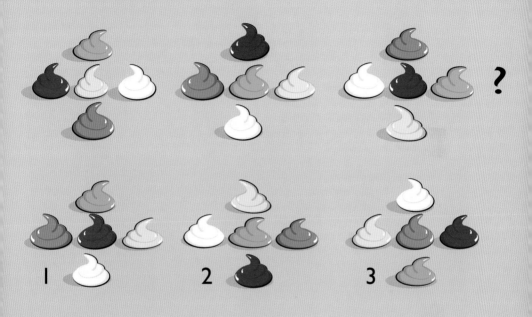

Which color combination has been substituted by the question mark?

A

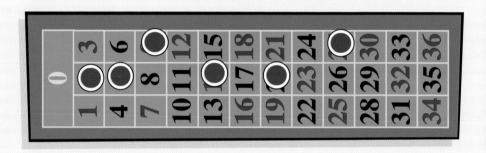

B

A Brian's gas stove has five plates. As usual, there's a Brian-like logic to the position of the knobs. Which should be the position (A–D) of the missing fifth knob?

Tip

B When Brian goes to a casino, he loves to play roulette. He always relies on his own successful system when he gambles. On which figure will he bet next?

Tip

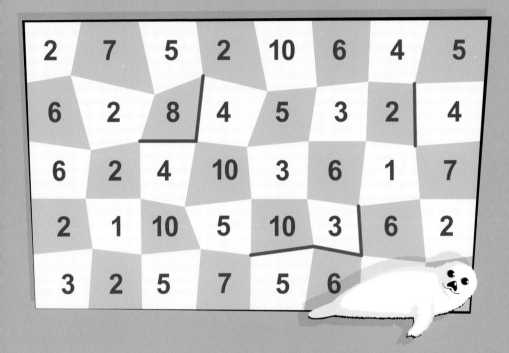

The young seal has begun marking off its territory. Continue its work until you obtain a closed circuit, while respecting the seal's logic.

Tip

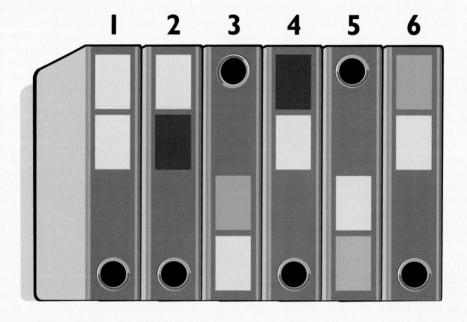

The secretary has her own system, so she immediately noticed that a binder was missing. In between which two binders should the missing binder be replaced?

Tip

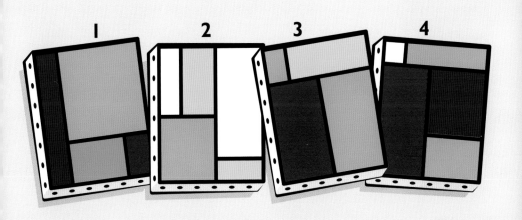

A painter inspired by the work of the famous Dutch painter Mondrian has painted three out of these four works himself. However, his paintbox only holds 6 colors. So which painting did he not paint himself?

Tip

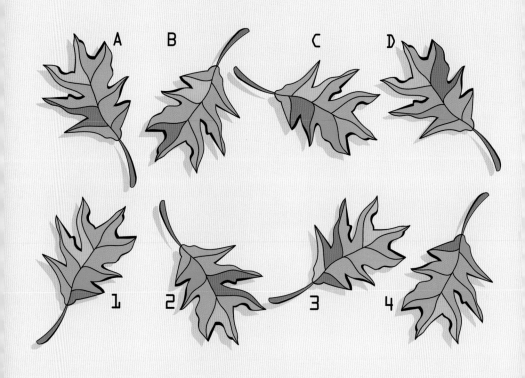

Leaves A–D need to be paired up with leaves 1–4,
but how? Your answer will look like this:
A3, B1, etc.

Tip

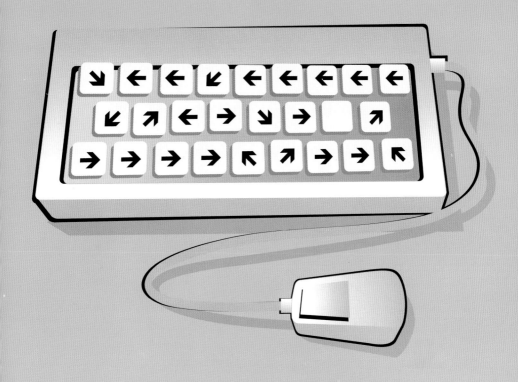

Which arrow is missing on the next to the last key on the second row? Indicate the orientation as: left, right, left upward, left downward, right upward, or right downward.

Tip

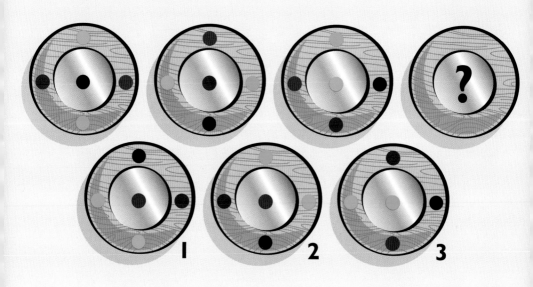

Which disc (1–3) has been replaced by a question mark?

Tip

A

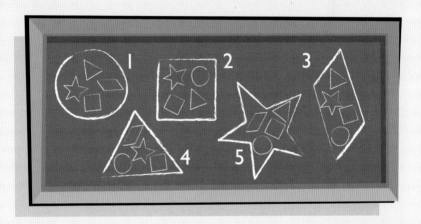

B

A Which missing letter will allow this lock to be opened?

B There is a mistake in one the groups (1–5) of figures. Which group are we talking about?

Tip

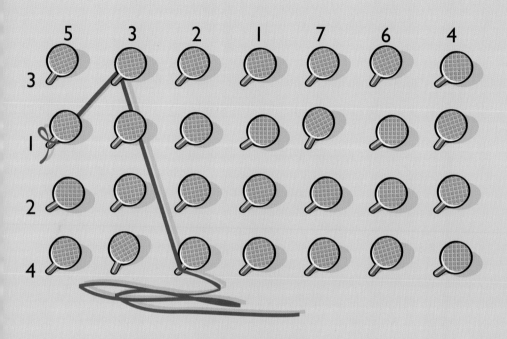

To which nail will the end of the rope be tied?

Tip

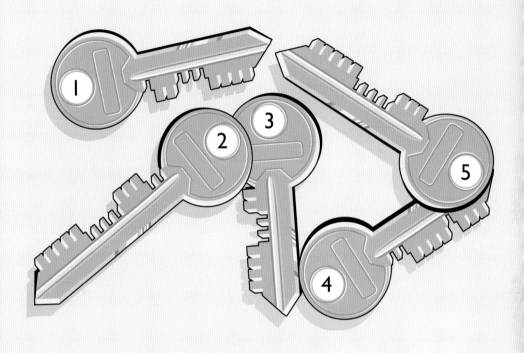

Key number 1 shows a succession of one notch, two teeth, three notches and four teeth. Which key (1–5) does not belong here?

Tip

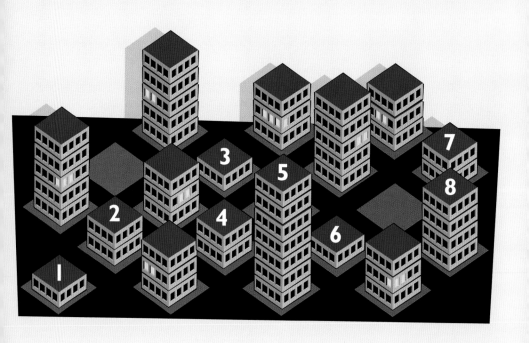

Wherever the light is still on, a burglary took place. Which building will the burglar next "honor" with a visit?

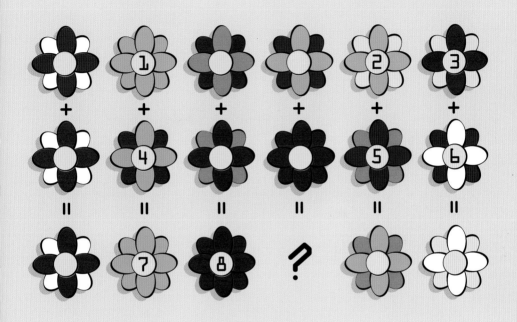

Study these flowers' dominent and recessive genetic traits. Which flower (1–8) has been replaced by a question mark?

Tip

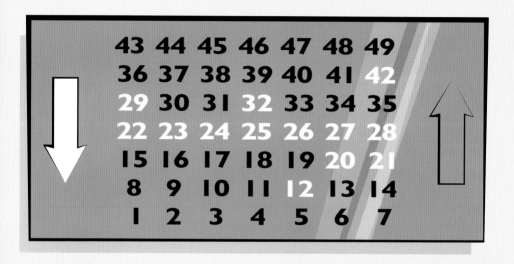

The elevator went down as far as the twelfth floor. The elevator stopped wherever the floor indications are lit. On which floor will the elevator stop next time?

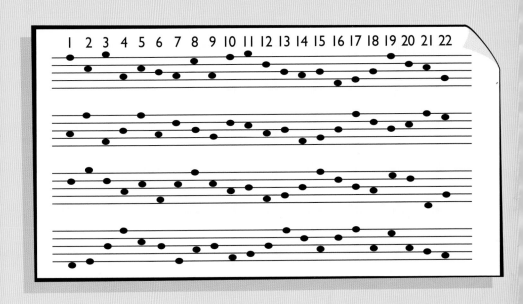

The refrain of this piece of music has seven notes and is found at a different place on each staff (row). Which note (1–22) does the refrain start with on the top staff?

On these paintings you can find two pairs of colors that are always used together. Which two pairs are we talking about? Your answers should follow a format such as 2/3 or 1/8.

Between which stacks should the bottom stack be placed in order to end up with a logical series of figures? On position 1, 2 or 3?

Tip

Not all the keys on this command panel that belong to the same group have lit up. How many keys still need to be pushed by the operator?

Tip

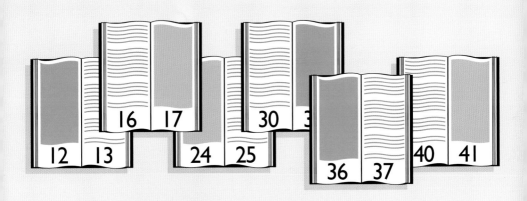

Based on the page numbers given, what is the next page on which a colored field will appear?

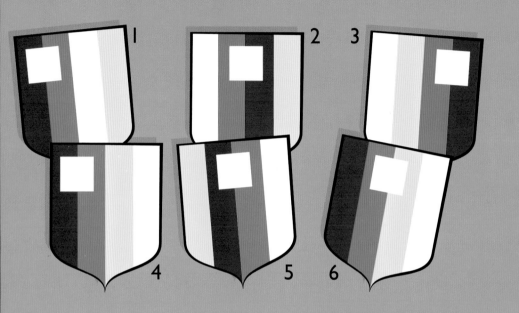

Which shield (1–6) does not belong here?

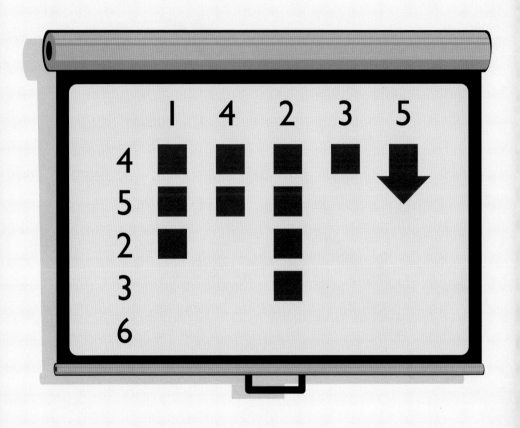

Where will line number five end?

Tip

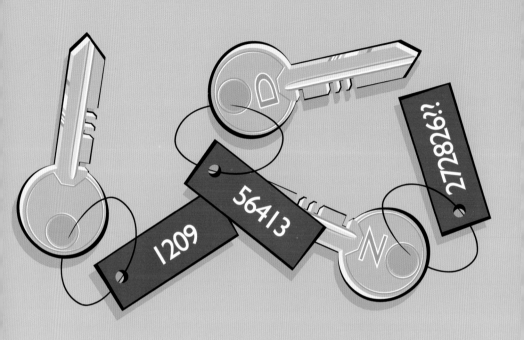

Complete the number on the last key ring.

Tip

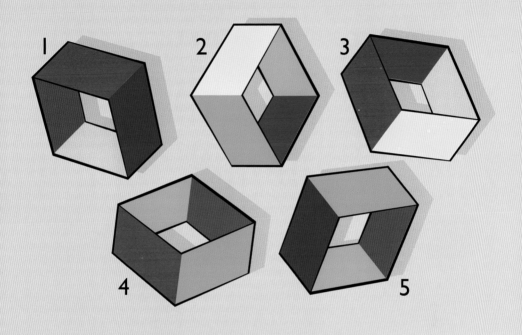

Which shape (1–5) is not identical to the other shapes?

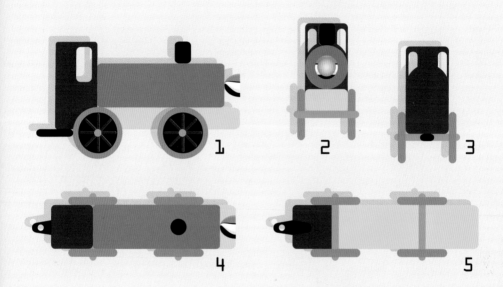

Which view (1–5) of the toy train is wrong?

Tip

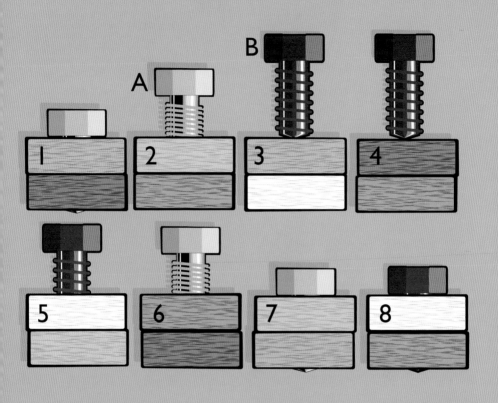

Screw bolts A and B are equally long, but their threads are different. Blocks of the same color have the same screw thread that takes only one type of bolt.
Which situation (1–8) is wrong?

Tip

In each stained glass window, a number of glass sections have been broken. These sections of glass come in three different sizes. Which window (1–4) must be sacrificed by the glassmaker in order to repair the other three windows without having to cut the glass?

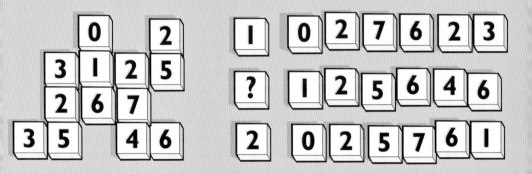

Which number has been replaced by
a question mark?

Tip

Can you make this big cube with identical smaller cubes that have six different colored faces?

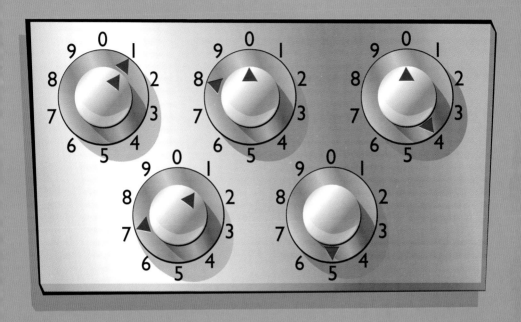

Each combination lock has two rings. Which number will the missing arrow be pointing at on the last lock?

Tip

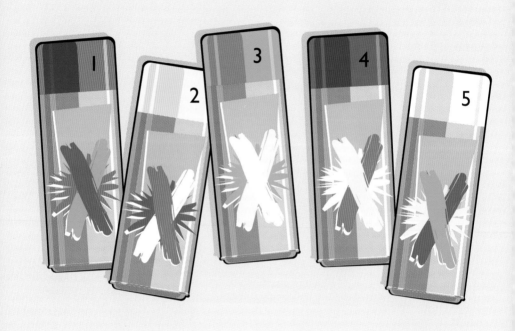

Only two caps have been put on the correct spray can.
Rearrange the order of the caps so that they are all
on the right cans.

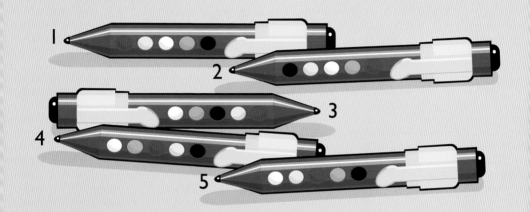

Which ballpoint pen (1–5) decorated with five colored dots does not belong in this set?

Tip

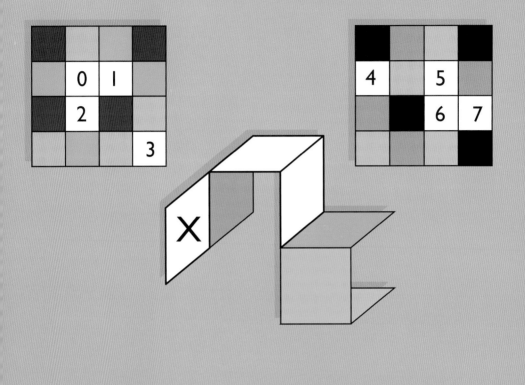

Find the base of the folded paper in the two grids, one of the grids being the front face and one the back face. Where will X (0–7) be found?

Tip

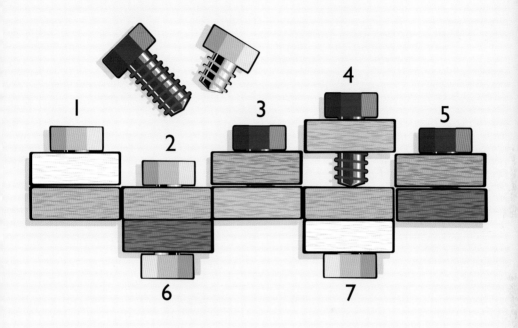

The two bolts are not of equal length. Blocks of the same color are identical. One kind of block does not have an opening. Which bolt (1–7) cannot possibly be in the right place?

Tip

Which work of art (1–5) does not fit in the collection?

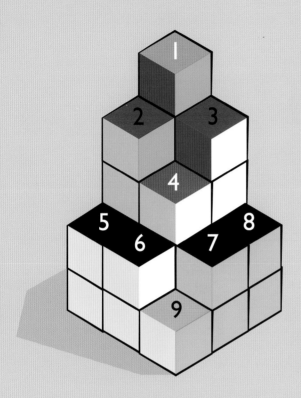

On which base (1–9) should the small cube be placed?

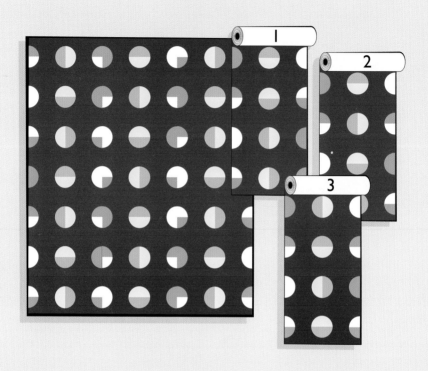

Which wallpaper roll (1–3) can you use to
continue the pattern?

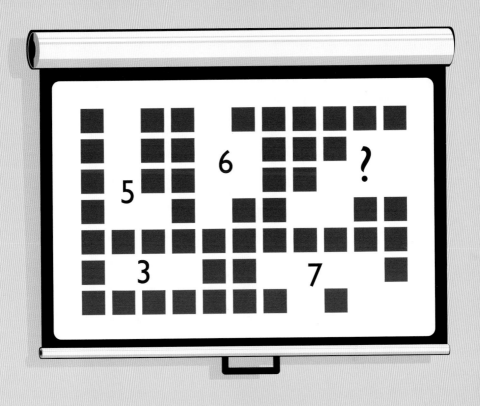

Which number has been replaced by
a question mark?

Tip

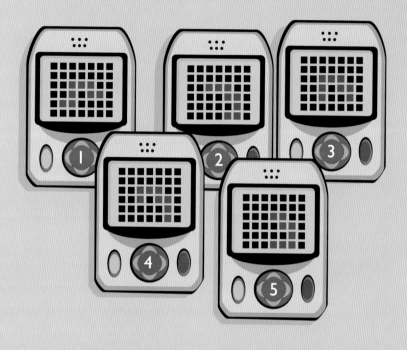

Put the five handheld computer games in the right order, starting with number 1.

Tip

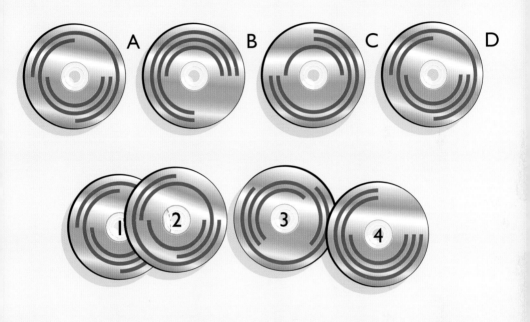

Which CD (1–4) will have to be put in which position (A–D)
in order to bring about a logical sequence?

Tip

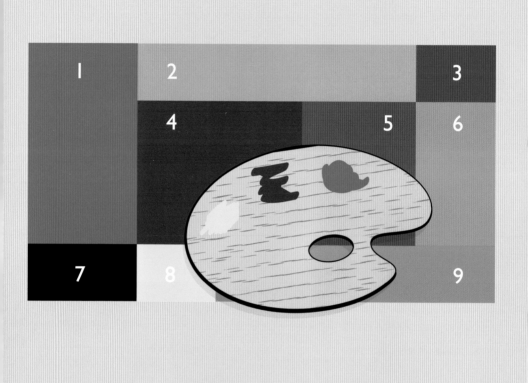

Which colors (1–9) cannot be obtained by mixing the colors on the painter's palette?

Tip

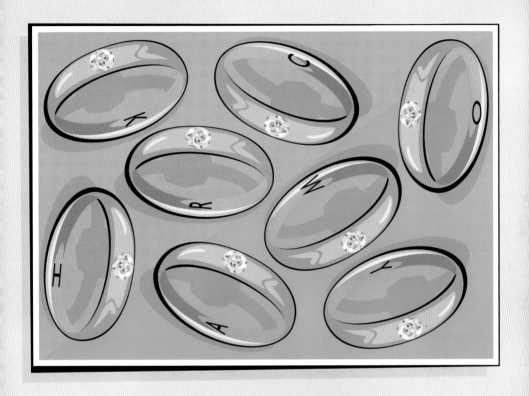

If wedding rings K and O go together, how should the other six rings be paired?

The child could not finish his drawing before bedtime. How (1–5) did he intend to finish the drawing with the question mark?

Tip

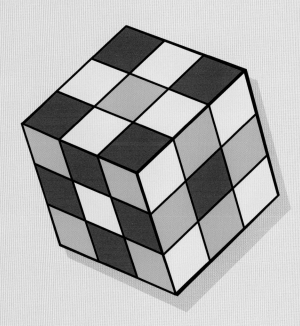

On each visible face of this cube you will notice the same pattern, but in three different color combinations. Using the same three basic colors, how many other color combinations can you make (in the same pattern, of course).

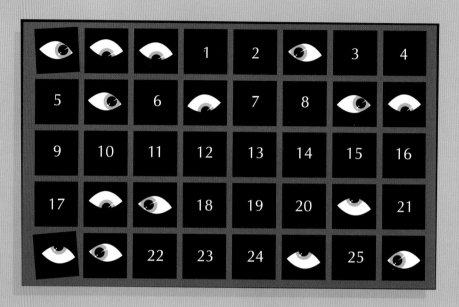

Where would you put an extra eye (1–25) in order to obtain a closed circuit, considering the viewing direction of the eyes and using all of the eyes?

Tip

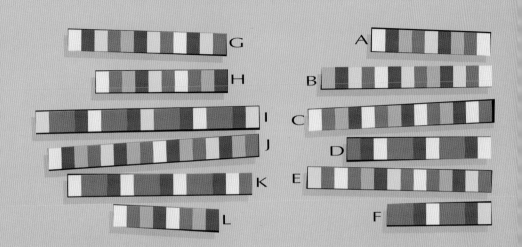

Six colored ribbons have been cut. Match the individual strips from the right-hand set with those from the left-hand set.

Tip

Which three letters have been hidden twice in this painting? Each letter has been made up of square planes and two colors.

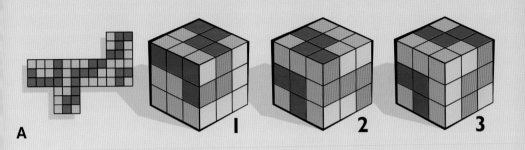

A Which cube do you get (1–3) when you fold
the ground plan?

B Which cube (1–5) is not identical to the other
four cubes?

Which numbered block (1, 4, or 7) belongs in the
empty space?

Tip

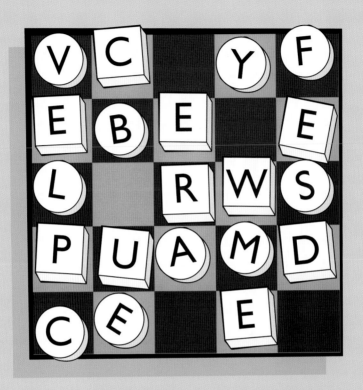

Delete five squares and five circles so that there is no more than one circle and/or one square in any row, column, or diagonal. The remaining letters constitute a word. Which word are we looking for?

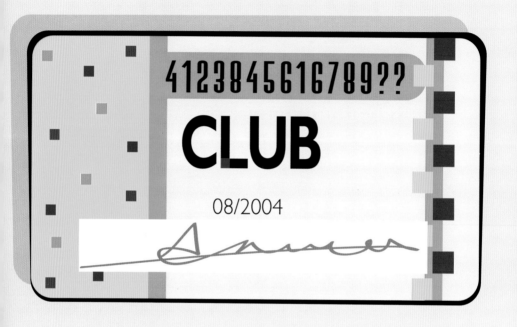

412384561678 9 ??

CLUB

08/2004

Which two numbers are missing on this
membership card?

The last black line is missing from the bar code on this bag of chips. The bar code is made up of lines of three different thicknesses: thin, normal, and thick. Which type of line is missing: a thin, normal, or thick line?

Tip

In a city where the streets are equally long and all cross at right angles, the taxi you are riding in turns left, right, or goes straight ahead at every corner. You suspect the driver is taking a longer route than necessary. If these are the directions the driver takes at each intersection, when did you find yourself back where you started?

Which two rows (A to L) must you switch in order to
obtain a pattern of repeating 4 by 4 squares that
starts in the upper left corner.

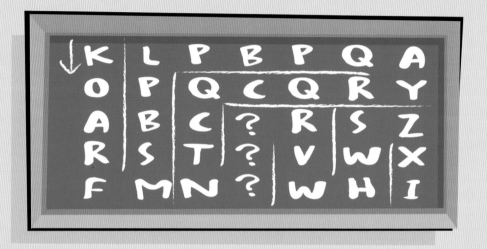

Start at the arrow and indicate which three letters are missing, in the order you pass them on the path.

Tip

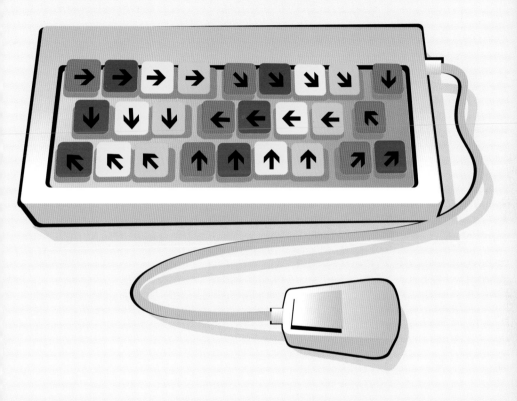

Which group of four arrows reveals a
logical mistake?

Tip

Which block (0–9) does not belong here?

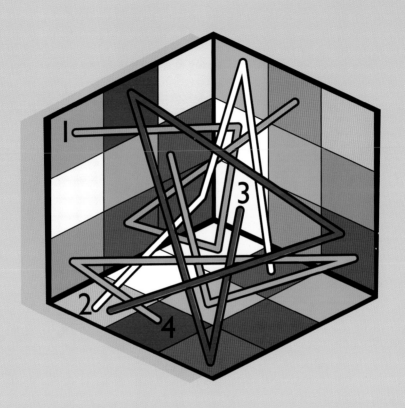

Which line (1–4) does not correctly link up the colored squares?

Tip

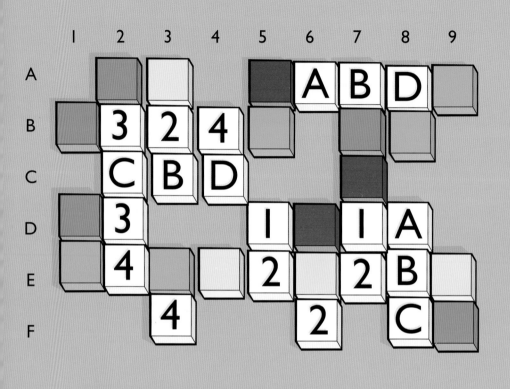

Indicate the coordinates (e.g., A6) of the letter cube that is not in the right place.

Tip

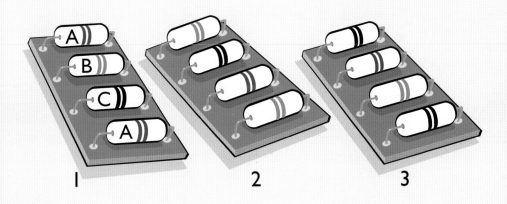

1   2   3

Only three different resistances were used in assembling these printing plates, and their order never changed. What will be the sequence (e.g., BCAB) of the resistances on the 100th printing plate, bearing in mind that an unnoticed mistake crept in on the 30th plate when two C-resistances were assembled in successive order?

Tip

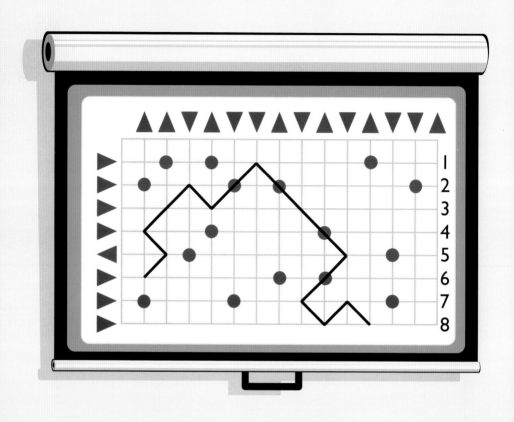

At what point (1–8) does the graph line end?

Tip

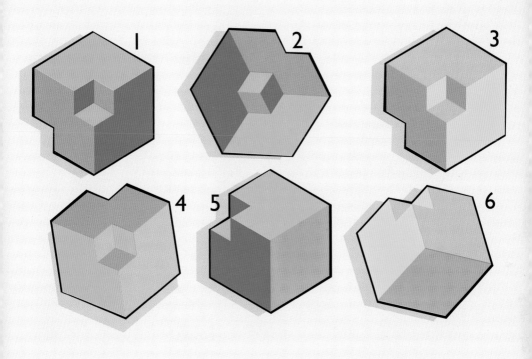

Only one picture (1–6) is not derived from the same cube.
Which one?

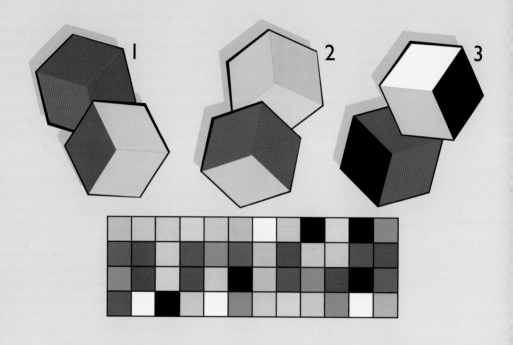

Here you see two profiles of three different cubes.
The base plan of which cube (1–3) has not been
integrated in the grid below?

Which cube (1–3) comes after cube C?

Tip

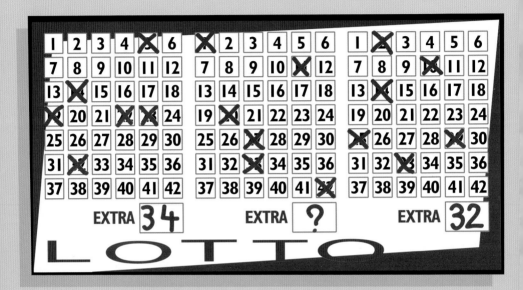

Which additional number is missing in the
second game above?

How many minutes of music are to be found
on the CD with the question mark?

Tip

Which beam (1–4) cannot be formed with the
ground plan of the same colors?

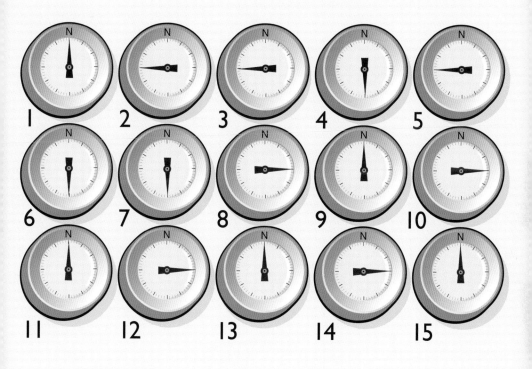

You are in a town that has only equally long streets that are always at right angles. You start at compass 1 and follow the direction until the end of the street. After which compass (1–15) will you be back in your starting place?

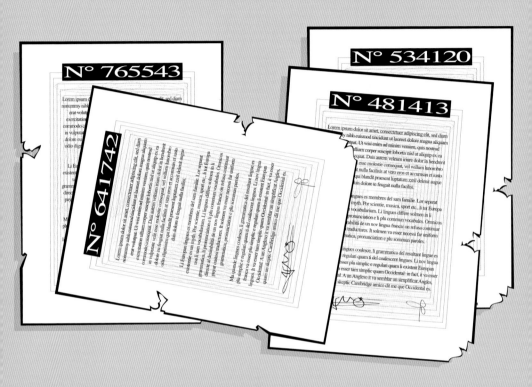

Which old share has been given a wrong number?

Which cube (1–9) is not in the right place?

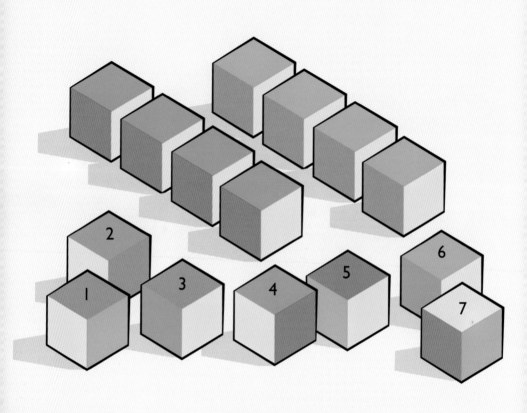

The two rows have been made up of identical cubes. Which loose cube (1–7) is not identical with the other cubes?

Four of the five pictures are of the same die. Which picture (1–5) does not come from that die?

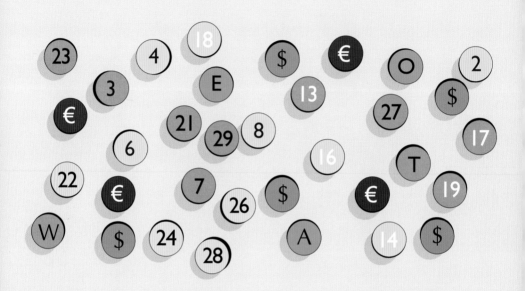

Which lottery ball does not fit in with
the logic of the set?

Tip

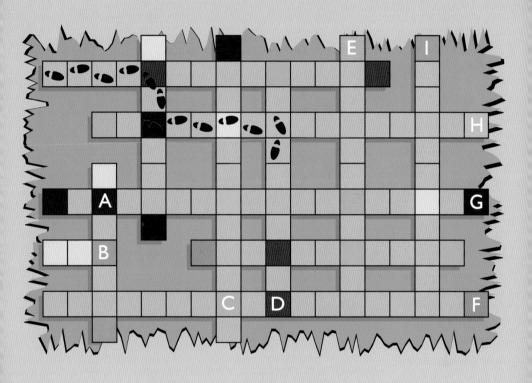

On which tile (A–I) will the walker change directions for the last time, provided he logically continues on the path on which he has started out?

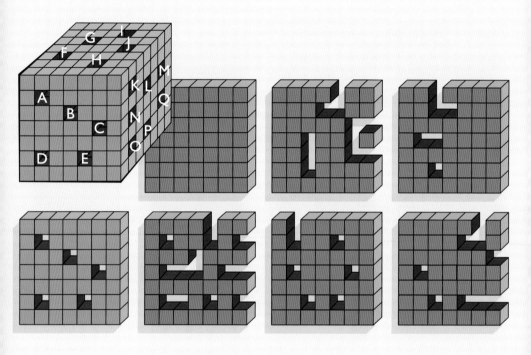

The cube above left is made up of the 7 blocks shown next to the cube. There are 7 tunnels in the cube (with different entrances and exits) and 3 recesses (which have only one entrance). Indicate with two letters the entrances and exits of the 7 tunnels — e.g., AD, GH, BC, ... — and the three letters for the recesses.

BrainStrains®

Great Color
Optical
Illusions

What's the trouble with Grandpa?

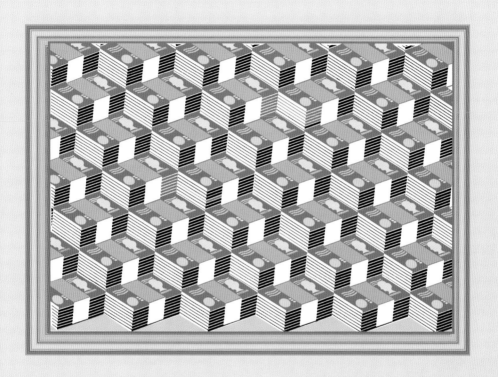

Are these stacks of bank notes sloping downwards
to the right or are they pointing down to the left?

This wavy "op art" shows a series of peaks and valleys.
What happens when you turn the page upside down?

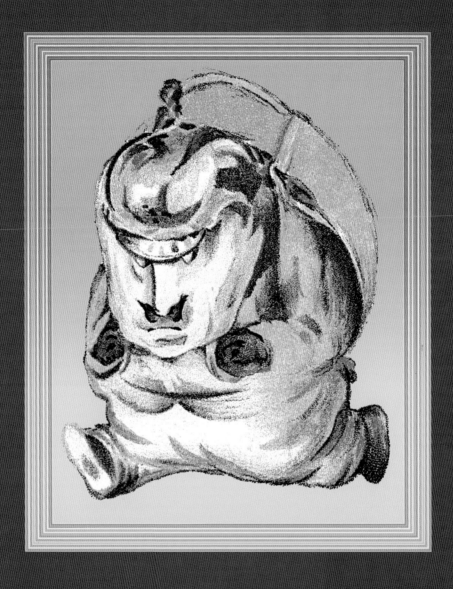

This illustration dates back to the First World War.
The Kaiser is on the run. What made him run?

Stare at the dot between the rabbit's eyes (try not to blink).
Count slowly to 30. Now look at a piece of white paper
or a blank wall. What do you see?

This is another World War 1 picture. Rotate the page in a counter clockwise direction. What happens to the steam engine?

A Bird
In The
The Hand

Read this well-known phrase. What does it say?
Are you sure?

BED	GREEN	DICE	RAIN
PEACE	EXCEDE	LION	DECK
BOX	CIRCLE	CODE	CHAIR
SWAN	CHICK	SMALL	CHOKED
DIXIE	DAISY	HOOD	CAT

Look at the reflection of this box in a mirror; all the words
are unreadable. Now turn the page upside down; what
happens to the letters in the orange squares?
How does this happen?

This is Garibaldi. Turn the page upside down and who does he become?

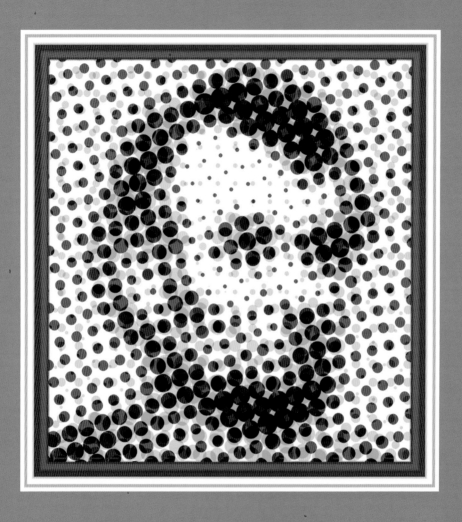

Who or what is represented with this series of dots?

Look at this page in a mirror. What happens to the words?
Why does it happen?

Here's a Victorian collection of barrels. Can you see anything else? What do you call a man that makes barrels?

The European puppet "Mr Punch" is looking for his wife Judy. Can you see where she is? Do you notice anything unusual about the way "punch" has been written?

In 1904, Serbia issued a famous "death mask" stamp: the profiles of Karageorge and Peter I Karageorgevich, when turned upside down, merge to form a death mask of the Serbian king Alexander I Obrenovich — who had been murdered in 1903 by Karageorgevich supporters. Can you find the hidden face?

Are the 3 dots on the inside or outside
of this triangle?

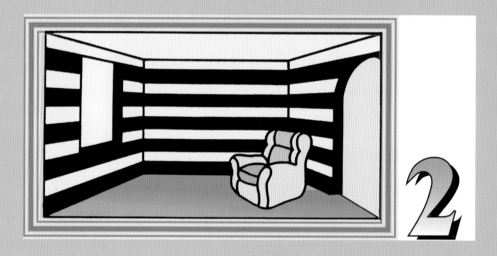

Why would anyone want to use vertical striped wallpaper as in room 1, or horizontal striped paper as in room 2?

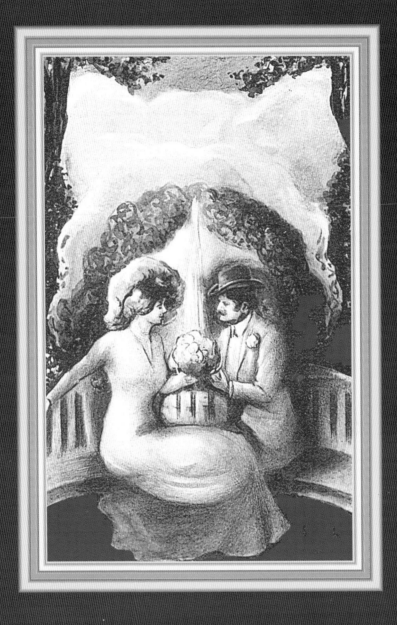

A Victorian print showing two young lovers in a garden setting — can you see who has got her "beady" eye on them?

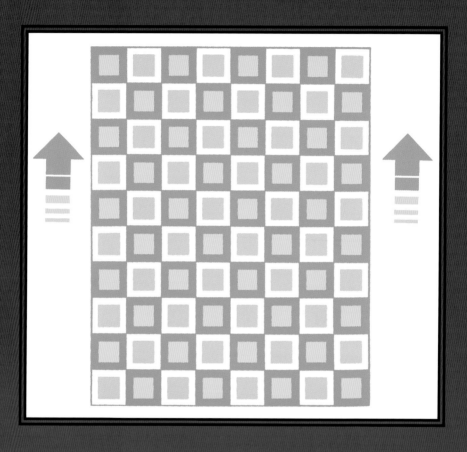

This design seems " higgledy-piggledy," but it is a regular pattern. Hold the page at eye level and look in the direction of the arrows. What happens?

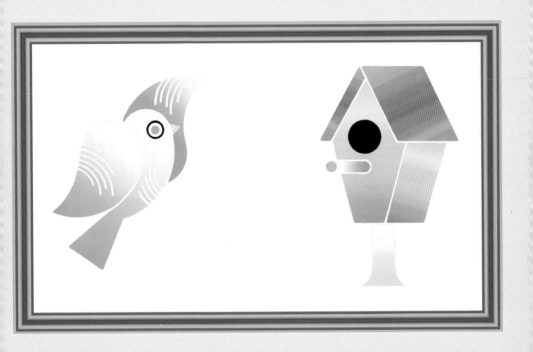

How can you get the bird to fly onto the perch?

Look very carefully at this illustration. Can you
see the animal?

What is this math teacher called?

Where are Jack and the Giants hiding?

This is called "The Man of a Thousand Faces."
Can you tell why?

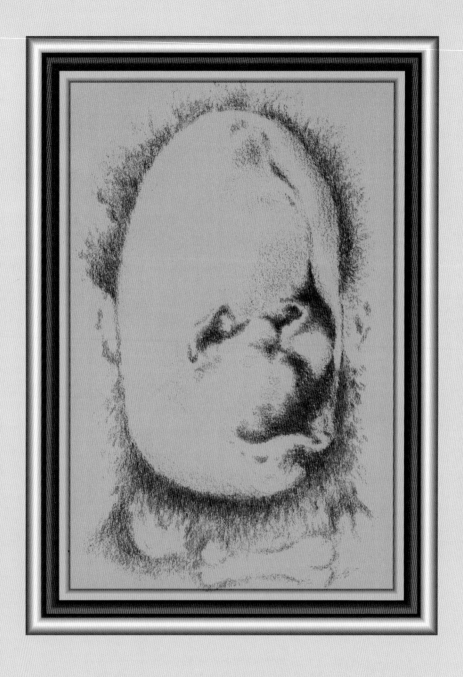

Is this weird picture animal, vegetable, or mineral?

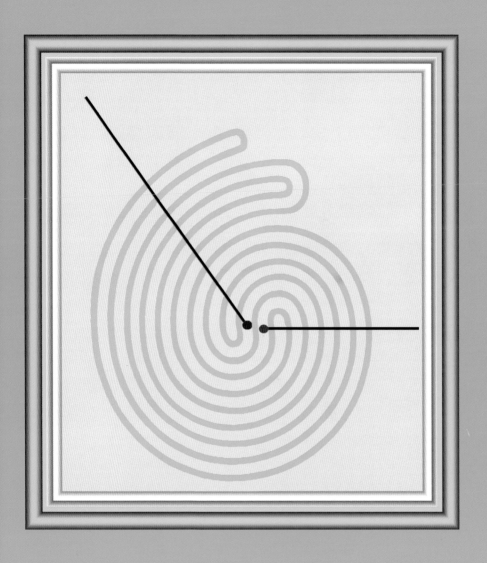

Which dot is on the inside? The blue or the red?

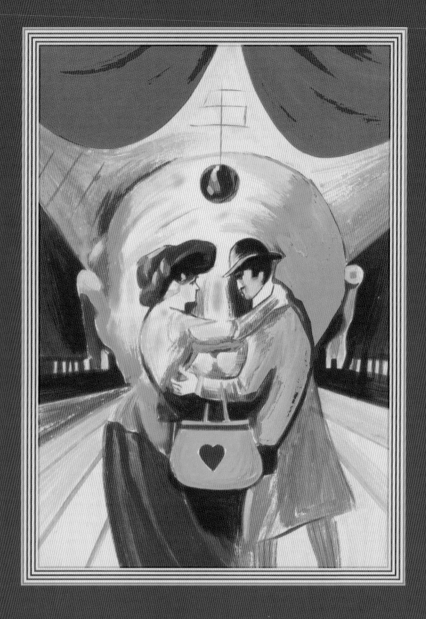

Look at this print close-up and you will see it as 2 people saying farewell. Now view the page from a long distance. What do you see?

Stare at this page for about 30 seconds — try not to blink.
Now look at a sheet of white paper or blank wall.
What do you see?

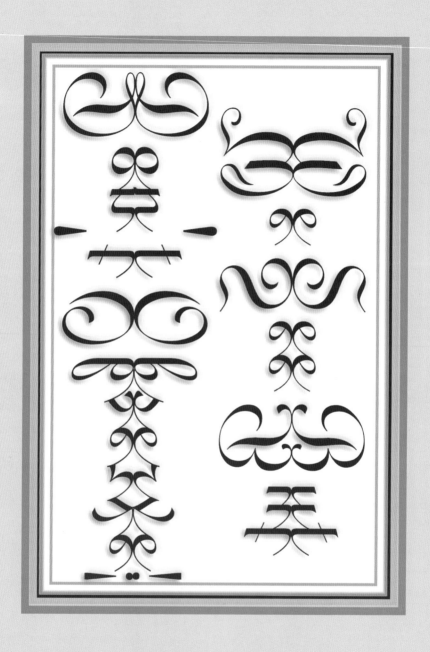

Can you discover the secret message that has been concealed in these hieroglyphics?

The landscape at sunset — can you see where
the giant is hiding?

The Magician is worried because he has
lost his rabbit. Can you find it?

This picture is titled "Three Heads under One Hat."
Can you see why?

Can you find the cows?

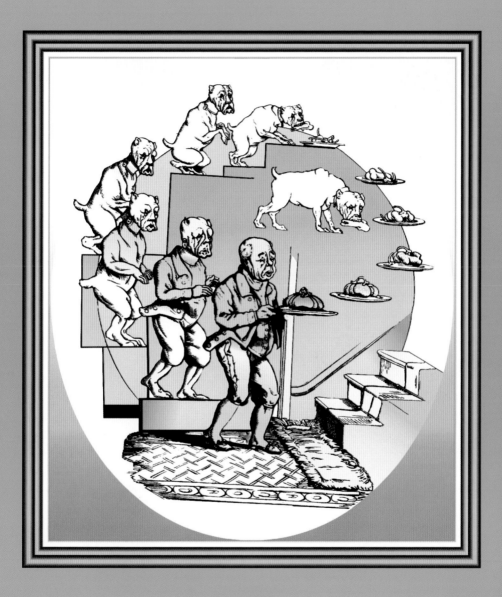

Can you see what's happening in this bygone print?

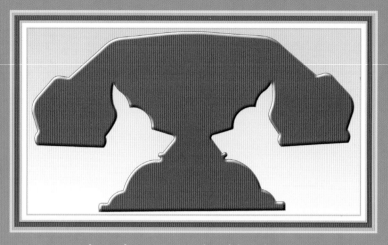

What do you see in this picture?

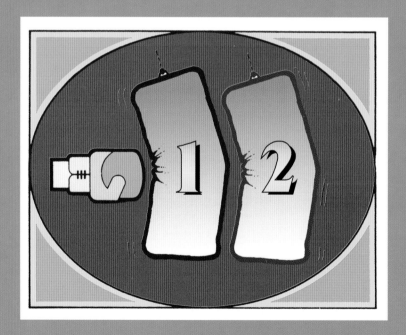

Which punching bag is bigger?

This juggler has two secret admirers.
Can you see them?

Slowly bring this page towards your face.
What happens?

What do you see in this picture?

This mathematical sum is wrong. With the use of a mirror, can you see what this is all about?

What's wrong with this spiral?

What do you see? Two people looking at each other
or a fancy vase?

This stamp was issued in 1944 — the artist made
a mistake in the design. Can you spot where
he went wrong?

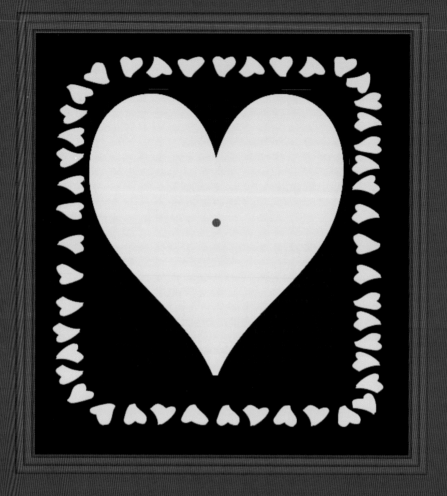

Stare at the small red dot for about 30 seconds,
Now look at a piece of white paper, blank wall
or ceiling. What do you see?

Slowly bring this page towards your face.
What happens to this man and woman?

This portrait was first published in Rome around
the year 1585. What else is special about it?

This is an amazing frog. When confronted with any sort of danger, it changes into a horse. Try looking at this sketch from different angles. Can you find the horse?

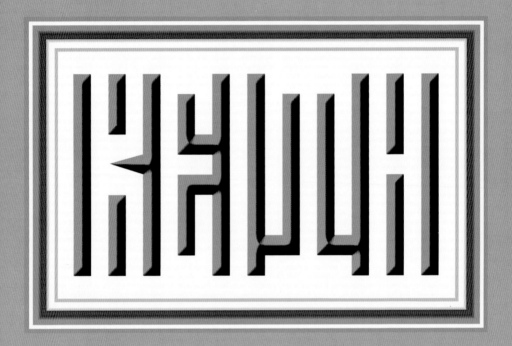

Can you find what word has been hidden in this set of lines?
Try looking at the page from a distance.

Finlay Dunn had a vaudeville act in England during the early part of the 20th century. Can you find his 3 faces?

Is this just a set of abstract shapes, or is it
a series of words?

What do you see in this Victorian print?

The winner always takes the first prize. The person who crosses the finish line at the tail end of the race comes in ＿＿＿. The missing word can be found in the illustration.

The soldier in this old French design
has a baby. Where is it?

Which square is bigger?

"Today & Tomorrow" is the title of this print, which is based on a Victorian original. It shows two young couples —but what happens when you view the page from a distance?

This print was issued during the Second World War.
The British Prime Minister Winston Churchill has been
hidden in the design. Can you find him?

What is this creature, a rabbit or a duck?

Can you find the man of the mountains?

One morning, a digital clock shows readout
No. 1, which is odd since it's well before noon.
Nearly two hours later, the clock shows readout
No. 2. Can you guess what is causing
the incorrect displays?

The mother is thinking about her son .
Can you see him?

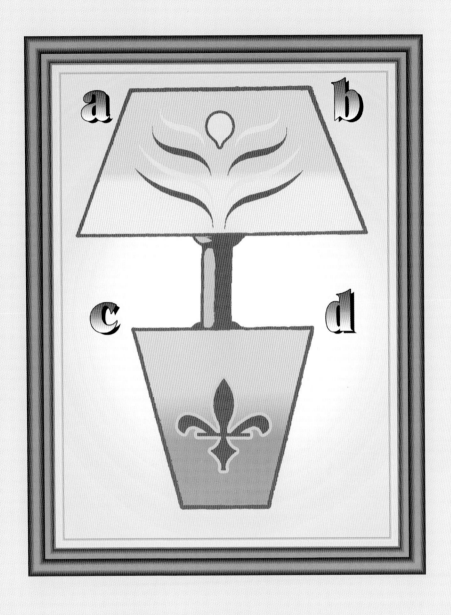

Is the top of the lamp shade longer than the top
of the lamp base?

Lord Byron

This Victorian print shows Lord Byron.
What's unusual about his portrait?

These two horses are dead, or are they?
How can you bring them back to life?

This stamp was issued in 1932. Can you see
the artist's mistake?

Hold this page about 3 inches in front of your face and gaze at the star and two clown hats. What happens?

What do you see here?
A young man or an old man?

Can you figure out what this "stained glass"
window shows?

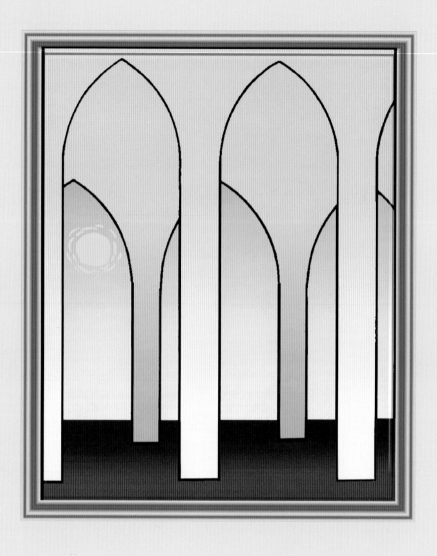

Do you think the sides of the cloister arches are disjointed? Or do they join up?

Are Abraham Lincoln and Benjamin Franklin
looking in different directions?

DO THESE LETTERS GO IN OR OUT ??????

Yes or no?

What is this a picture of ?

Can you identify what these shapes
mean or represent?

We read this sign as THE CAT, but examine the middle letters of each word and you will see they are identical. Yet we see the letters as H in THE and A in CAT. Why is that?

Hold this page about 5 inches in front of you.
Close your right eye and focus on the boy with your
left eye. Slowly bring the page closer to your eyes.
What happens at a certain distance?

Here is another print which goes back to World War I.
An inverted image shows a clergyman and the Kaiser.
Why does it have two captions?

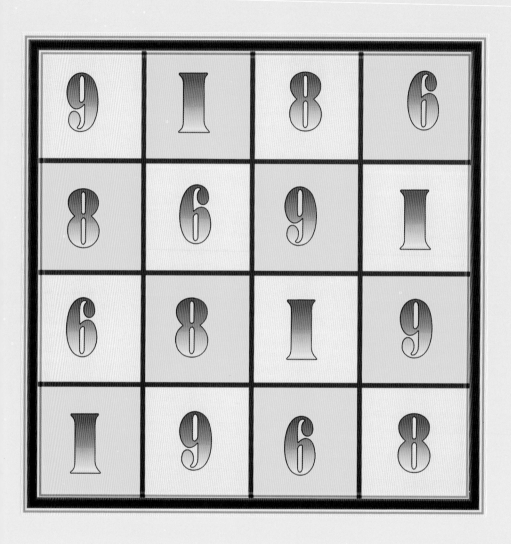

What's so special about this set of numbers?

FUNEX?
SVFX
FUNEM?
SVFM
OKVFMNX42!

Can you read and understand this message?

Which animals do we have here, two rabbits or
two ducks or a duck and a rabbit?

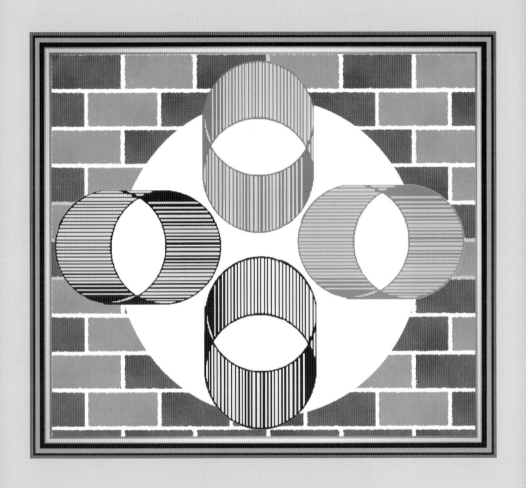

Which way are the tubes facing?

How many candles do you see here?

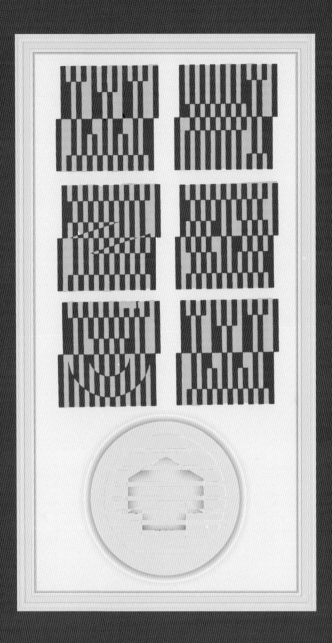

This "op art" series of panels contains a secret
message. Can you decipher it ?

BrainSnack® Puzzles Tips

Page 10
A Square patterns
B 1 and 2

Page 11
10

Page 13
1929+(?+?) = 1940

Page 16
Number of grid squares

Page 19
Look at adjoining
flower petals.

Page 20
Colors around black

Page 21
7, 8, 9

Page 22
17+? = 20+? = 26

Page 23
A The sum

Page 24
Orange is 4

Page 25
Count the red rings.

Page 26
Look on the barrel.

Page 27
Gray is the most expensive.

Page 28
Divide by 7.

Page 30
10 and 15

Page 35
+2 and x2

Page 32
Count the cubes per color.

Page 33
Look on a diagonal.

Page 34
From 1 to 5

Page 36
A Multiply with the largest number and divide by the smallest.

B Circumference of a circle.

Page 37
Next cell

Page 39
16+9 = 25

Page 41
Counterclockwise

Page 42
Start at the corners.

Page 43
169+(?+?+?) = 185

Page 44
A Count all the arrows.
B Sum of the figures/100.

Page 45
Letter = number

Page 48
Sum x 3

Page 49
Follow two colors.

Page 50
From 2 to 3

Page 51
The tangent planes

Page 54
Color = direction.

Page 56
+2

Page 58
The second letter

Page 59
Before and after bend

Page 60
247.9 km

Page 61
The sum per row.

Page 63
From 0 to 9

Page 65
Add up two figures.

Page 66
Mirror.

Page 67
6?6 = 4?3

Page 69
Odd numbers

Page 71
Difference between zone numbers

Page 72
Follow the colors.

Page 74
Ribbons and balls

Page 75
A The next letter
B x/100

Page 76
Total above and below

Page 80
10% more

Page 81
Formula for distance
relates to column
number.

Page 82
A formula per color

Page 83
Start at the corners.

Page 84
5+3 = 8

Page 85
Mirror image

Page 86
Color of the big ball

Page 88
An imaginary square

Page 89
Valve

Page 91
Difference in stars
per color.

Page 92
Count black confetti

Page 93
Color sequence

Page 96
Red and yellow

Page 97
1x1, 2x2, 3x3...

Page 98
11

Page 99
Red, yellow, and purple

Page 101
1, 2, 3, 4, 5

Page 102
A Time difference.
B Impossible

Page 103
Number of blocks

Page 106
Number = letter

Page 107
Decimal sequence

Page 108
Follow the figures on
the keyboard.

Page 109
3 hunters

Page 110
3 keys do not function

Page 112
Ascending series

Page 113
Diagonal

Page 114
Rounded corners

Page 120
A The two previous
   lamps

Page 121
Fold next to red

Page 122
The red blocks

Page 123
A star

Page 124
2 colors

Page 125
Folding rule

Page 126
25 pills

Page 128
Follow one color.

Page 132
A 1, 2, 3, 4
B 2 (+3) = 5 (+4) =
   9 (+5) = 14...

Page 133
Division by two

Page 134
Color order

Page 135
Black and white are
also colors.

Page 136
A complete green leaf

Page 137
Endless loop

Page 138
Follow black.

Page 139
B The large
surrounding form

Page 140
6

Page 141
Notches and teeth

Page 143
Red dominates purple.

Page 147
Follow one figure.

Page 148
Look beneath the keys.

Page 151
1 till 2

Page 152
D = 1(+4) = 5,
2(+4) = 6...

Page 154
Wheel axle

Page 155
Block 5 has thread B.

Page 157
Around the figure

Page 176
Second and fourth ball

Page 159
Even = 0

Page 161
Second and fourth dots

Page 162
Mirror

Page 163
The brown block

Page 167
The missing blocks

Page 168
1 pixel

Page 169
–90° +90° 180°

Page 170
Mixed colors

Page 172
Sun, feet and hands

Page 174
An eye looking to
the right

Page 175
Watch the colors.

Page 178
Intersection

Page 181
The numbers are
irrelevant.

Page 184
The other side of
the line

Page 185
90°

Page 187
Color sequence

Page 188
Figures, letters,
and colors

Page 189
Repetition after 3
printing plates

Page 190
Circle = repeat
movement.

Page 193
120°

Page 195
(6 x 11) – 15 = 51

Page 202
Watch colors and
prints of balls.

BrainSnack® Puzzles Answers

Page 10

A Cake number 2. All the other cakes have been decorated with square patterns in white chocolate.

B The pattern being repeated is minus 1 and then divide by 2. The first cake has 15 lines − 1 = 14 / 2 = 7 − 1 = 6 / 2 = 3 − 1 = 2. The next cake will have two chocolate lines.

Page 11

The total number of white dots on the front and back sides of each group is 10. Consequently the last mushroom is missing one white dot.

Page 12
Slice number 4.

Page 13
1944. The connoisseur takes the last two digits of the year of vintage of a bottle, adds them to the figure of the year and this results in the year of vintage of the next bottle: 1914 + (1 + 4) = 1919 + (1 + 9) = 1929 + (2 + 9) = 1940 + (4 + 0) = 1944.

Page 14
The correct answer is BRIAN.

Page 15
Pralines 3 and 5.

Page 16
4532. Each number is made up by the grid squares one can count in front of, above, behind, and under the number.

Page 17
Piece D.

Page 18
28 intersections. One route is from A to B - C - G - I
- H - L - J - K - E - D - F.

Page 19
Flower 4. The colors of the adjoining flower petals
always match.

Page 20
Ball number 3. The colored faces encircling the black
face are ordered in the opposite direction.

Page 21
4. Each number consists of three two-digit numbers.
The sum of the figures that make up the two-digit
numbers is always one higher than the sum of the
previous two-digit number. On the first ticket we read
19, 83 and 66. The sum of the figures that
make up the two-digit numbers is 10 (1 +9),

11 (8 +3) and 12 (6 +6). The last ticket starts
with the figure 7 (4 +3). The last two-digit number
will consequently need to have a sum of 9. The
missing figure is 4.

Page 22
47. Every day the additional number of yellow
cards is the next multiple of 3. 17 (+3) = 20
(+6) = 26 (+9) = 35 (+12) = 47.

Page 23
A 5. The sum of all the figures around the center
      equals the figure in the center.
B With tiles 2, 3 and 4 it is possible to reconstitute
      the pattern on tile 3. This is impossible with tile 1.

Page 24
B. The color values are: 1 black. 2 purple, 3 blue,
4 orange, and 5 yellow.

Page 25
As there are only four red rings, you can only make
four logos.

Page 26
Only gun number 6 has a sight on its barrel.

Page 27
A blue ski boot costs 8 units.
A yellow one costs 13 − 8 = 5.
A red boot costs 15 − 5 = 10.
A green boot costs 17 − 10 = 7.
It follows that the gray boot costs 23 − 7 − 5 = 11.

Page 28
Six moons. Count up all the moons and then divide the number by seven.

Page 29
Liquid 4.

Page 30
7. The sum of all the horizontal squares always equals 10 and the sum of each group of vertical squares always equals 15.

Page 31
5. The number of the green microbes increases by two each time, whereas the purple microbes multiply tin number each time.

Page 32
1 cube. The number of black and purple cubes equals the number of red cubes.

Page 33
14 and 1. On any diagonal from upper left to lower right you always obtain short series of increasing numbers.

Page 34
31245. All the other combinations are rotations of the series 12345.

Page 35
60°C.

Page 36
A ((8+6)x9)/1−3=123
B 1. This is the beginning of the number pi:
   3.14159265359....

Page 37
Nucleus 2. The cell nuclei always have the color
of the next cell.

Page 38
89%. The percentage is increased by 22 each time.

Page 39
2 or 23. The highest number of a series of a
similar color equals the sum of all the other
numbers. The number for the series is:
9 + 16 = 25. Consequently 21 should be in
a series with 2 and 23. 2 + 21 = 23.

Page 40
5. The figures on two out of three balls, both on a
horizontal and on a vertical axis, constitute the figure
to be found on the third ball.

Page 41
Sector A. Per row and from left to right, the triangular pattern is moving one sector counter clockwise.

Page 42
In net square H. Starting at the left upper corner, the goals are scored in the next (clockwise) corner each time. Moreover, the ball hits the net at a distance of 1, 2, 3, 4, and 5 squares from the respective corners and on a diagonal line starting in that corner. It follows that the sixth goal will be scored at a distance of 6 squares from the right upper corner.

Page 43
The height is increased each time by the sum of the figures of the number. This gives you:
218 + (2 + 1 + 8) = 229.

Page 44

A Ten arrows. Each time the archer is shooting the total number of arrows he has put into the preceding target into the circles of the next target.

B Each next jump is increased with the number of centimeters equal the sum of the figures that make up the previous jump but divided by 100. So his next jump will take him 7.85 + ((7 + 5 + 8)/100) = 8.05 meters.

Page 45

BH. Just replace the numbers of the bobsleds by the letters that occupy the corresponding place in the alphabet.

Page 46

62 seconds. The formula is: 13 + (1 x 3) = 16 + (1 x 6) = 22 + (2 x 2) = 26 + (2 x 6) = 38 + (3 x 8) = 62.

Page 47
Paddle number 4.

Page 48
15. The sum of all the ski lifts of a previous row is multiplied by three in order to calculate the total of lifts for the next row. The sum of the cable lifts equals 4. The sum of the egg lifts equals 4 x 3 = 12. The sum of the chair lifts equals 12 x 3 = 36. The sum of the tow lifts should be 36 x 3 = 108. It follows that 15 tow lifts are missing.

Page 49
At point 5. He only does the black and red tracks.

Page 50
Normally all the connections go from the top of one chip to the bottom of the next. This is not the case for chip B.

Page 51
Crystal 1. All the tangent planes have the same color.

Page 52
Piece A.

Page 53
In measuring glasses 1 and 4, the salt water ratio is the same. However, since the volume of water in glass 1 is higher, the volume of salt will also be higher.

Page 54
At point B. The previous print lines show that the dot color denotes direction to take: black to the right, white to the left, red straight ahead.

Page 55
9472. After the first turn of the lock, each figure is moved one position further. The next turn, two positions. Then three positions, and the fourth time four positions.

Page 56
6439517. Each time a figure is introduced, it is increased by two.

Page 57
10. The series of temperatures reads this way: +5 −9 +8, +8 −9 +5.

Page 58
In Orléans. The riders visit the cities in alphabetical order, ignoring the first letter of each city name.

Page 59
43. The number is calculated as follows: the figure of the bend before the bend that is missed represents the tens and the figure for the bend after the missed bend the units. 4 and 3 constitute 43.

Page 60
Place number 7. The rider has had a puncture at each place indicated by the figures of the number that indicates the kilometers of the ride.

Page 61
25. The sum of the numbers on the back of the riders in each row is always equal to 25.

Page 62
At number 56. The riders get a drink at each number the first digit of which is smaller than the second.

Page 63
The total price is 747. All the figures from 0 to 9 are used and along the diagonal the figures are increased by 1 each time. The first number, consequently, is 170.

Page 64
8. The green square can represent five. 5 + 5= 10. In the third column, the 6 can only be the result of 5+1. In the second column, we thus get 5 + 1 + 1 (carried over from the first column) = 7. In the fourth column, we get 7 + 1 = 8.

Page 65
5. Each consecutive number in a row is added together and the sum placed below them.

Page 66
Protein A. The DNA string reads the same backwards as forwards.

Page 67
Blood sample C. In the case of all the other blood samples, the result of an operation with the two left hand figures equals the result of an operation with the two right hand figures.
6 + 6 = 4 x 3, 15 − 1 = 7 x 2, 16/2 = 5 + 3.

Page 68
11 bandages.

Page 69
B. The cells tend to cluster in odd numbers.

Page 70
8. The sum of the temperature indications on the left and right thermometers starting from the middle each time equals 20: far left (6) + far right (14) = 20; second left (11) + second right (9) = 20, etc.

Page 71
741702. The difference between the zone (area code) numbers (09 + 2 = 11; 11 − 8 = 03; 03 + 5 = 08) is reflected by the decimals in the phone numbers.

Page 72
D. The colors on this ball have been applied in a different way.

Page 73
Bag 4. The colors on all the other bags match the color of the contents of the bag.

Page 74
Party hat 3. All the hats have exactly the same
number of ribbons and balls of the same color with
all the other ribbons matching the bill of the hat,
excepting only hat #3, where the other ribbons do not
match the bill.

Page 75
A   Champagne. Just replace each letter by the next
      letter of the alphabet.
B   0.23. The sum of the figures on each bell divided
      by 100 indicates the clapper weight.

Page 76
11. The number of snowballs in every place of
the middle row equals the sum of the number
of snowballs above and below.

Page 77
1. The number of closed windows on each floor
corresponds to the number of the floor.

Page 78
Carnaval.

Page 79
On stack 4. Pink boxes are always stacked on blue
boxes, blue on orange, and orange on pink.

Page 80
1825, and this is why: 1265 (+10% of 1200) =
1385 (+10% of 1300) = 1515 (+10% of 1500) =
1665 (+10% of 1600) = 1825.

Page 81
They should both read 4. The formula goes like this:
(distance of the black track x 2) − place in the row =
distance of the red track. (Distance of the red
track x 2) − place in the row = distance of the
blue track. The fourth distance thus becomes:
(4 x 2) − 4 = 4 (red track) and (4 x 2) − 4 =
4 (blue track).

Page 82
10. A red dot indicates an increase of 4, a black dot 3, and a blue dot reduces the number by 6. The direction in which the increases and decreases should be made is indicated by the arrows

Page 83
E4. Following the rectangle contours counterclockwise, we find the three crosses, respectively, 2, 3, and 4 squares from the corner. The fourth cross will consequently be at 5 squares from the right upper corner.

Page 84
Number 17. There are three different teams and within each team the sum of the figures of the rider numbers is identical. Rider number 17 belongs to the team with numbers 25, 52 and 133. His number is wrong because the sum of the figures of the numbers of the other riders in his team equals 7.

Page 85
7B. The ball hits its mirror image in the net.

Page 86
Duck number 3. With all the other ducks the color of the big ball on their cap is the same as the color of the majority of the small balls.

Page 87
4. The red rectangle in the top center does not appear on cabins A and B.

Page 88
Piece 7. Pieces of confetti that have the same color are situated on the four corners of an imaginary square.

Page 89
Beachball 5. The valve is on the wrong side.

Page 90
Glass 3.

Page 91
11. This is why. The number of yellow stars equals $11 (-4) = 7 (-3) = 4 (-2) = 2 (-1) = 1$.

The number of red stars is: 1 (+4) = 5 (+3) = 8 (+2) = 10 (+1) = 11.

Page 92
Four. You count 7 black confetti among those thrown. Two thrown bags of 1 type and one thrown bag of type 2 accounts for 3 of the black confetti. You would have thrown at least 7 − 3 = 4 bags of type 3.

Page 93
Rank three. The ranking order is determined by the color of the feather. The ranking order is indicated on the hat of Prince Carnival (hat 1) by the colored balls: black − grey − white.

Page 94
Candy egg 4. The basic color of the wrapping matches the color of the chocolate filling. The color of the stripes on the wrapping corresponds to the type of chocolate: white = purple stripes; milk chocolate = yellow stripes; and dark chocolate = red stripes. Egg 4's yellow stripes should be red.

Page 95

8. All the Easter rabbits on a card that has the same sum of the digits of the figures on the card also have the same color. Example: the sum of the digits on the cards of the gray rabbits is 6 every time. Each color thus corresponds to a figure. Out of the four remaining empty cards, only card number 13 (sum = 4) has not yet been allocated to a color. It follows that you will need one more color than the ones you see now.

Page 96

Water ring K. Two red and two yellow colors in opposing rings are alternatively linked. He will respect this logic best if he takes the following route: A - B - D - J - I - O - N - H - G - F - L - K.

Page 97

Surfer number 3457622. On the winner's sail is a figure 1 one time. Second place has twice the figure 2 on his sail. Third has three times 3, fourth four times 4, and fifth five times the figure 5.

Page 98
Protection factor 43. If we organize the tubes in an ascending order, the difference between the tubes is 11 each time: 10, 21, 32, 43, 54.

Page 99
Beachball 6. All the other beachballs have a red, yellow, and purple face.

Page 100
This is the right solution.

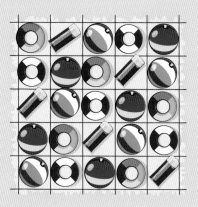

Page 101
One more blue band. After each blue band you get
first 1, then 2, then 3, then 4, and finally 5 bands
of another color.

Page 102
A   00:42. A difference of one hour and ten minutes.
B The time indication of 36:59 cannot possibly figure
    on the display of a clock.

Page 103
Figure C is the only one to be made of 18 blocks. All
the other figures needed 19 blocks.

Page 104
"I LOVE YOU"

Page 105
Piece number 1.

Page 106
17. The number of the keys coincides with their place in the alphabet. Keys 1, 2, and 3 have already been replaced by the letters A, B, and C. Q being the 17th letter.

Page 107
Each decimal sequence has been given a certain color. So the color for key 19 will be the same as the one on key 16.

Page 108
943. Follow the figures on the keyboard from above left to down right.

Page 109
You need a minimum of 3 hunters and they will stand guard on spots E, F, and I.

Page 110
Figure 2. Keys 3, 4, and 9 do not function properly, which is why those figures cannot be displayed.

Page 111
Figure number 3. The analysis of the previous series tells us that the ascending order of superiority is 4, 5, 2, 1, 3.

Page 112
7. The reasoning is as follows: 1, 2, 3 (2+1), 4, 5 (3+2), 6 (4+2), 7 (3+2+2).

Page 113
7. The sum of the diagonal figures is the same on each scoreboard.

Page 114
Stack number 2. All the other glass stacks have rectangles with rounded corners.

Page 115
Piece number 4

Page 116
3142. There is a double indication: first, the first letters in alphabetical order (A–Z) and, next, the first figures on the plates in order of importance.

Page 117
Six doors.

Page 118
Square number 2. Each column uses squares of three different colors and each time one, two, and three blocks are of the same color. The three squares of the same color take the color of the single block from the previous column.

Page 119
Space 2. Black cars are always stationed between two white cars and in front of a red car.

Page 120
A 2875 hours. The number of hours a lamp burns
    equals the average number of hours the two
    previous lamps burn.
B 5. The sum of the figures on the digital display of
    each clock equals 14.

Page 120
Strip 3. The other strips all fold next to the
red space.

Page 122
Situation 6. Only the red blocks have not been given
threaded holes.

Page 123
Form 6. All the forms that precede a star are part of
the set.

Page 124
Strip 4. All the other strips have outer lines of the
same color.

Page 125
Strip 2. All the other strips have been assembled in such a way that they can be folded up like a folding ruler.

Page 126
None. After five days, the patient has taken all of his 25 pills.

Page 127
You can use a maximum of 29 rods. Consequently you need 28 units.

Page 128
Block 6. A block cannot have a red and purple face.

Page 129
Combination 3. The colors rotate through the stack from top to bottom, with the color of the bottom shape moving to the top.

Page 130
If you swap two and three, you obtain diagonal blocks of the same color. Those are also the only two windows that can be moved, as they do not constitute a corner.

Page 131
Combination 3. The colors rotate one space clockwise until they reach the top of the cross, when they drop down to the center, then move one space to the right and rotate clockwise again.

Page 132
A Knob D. Brian gave knob A one turn to the left. He gave knob B two turns to the left. He gave knob C three turns to the left. So he will have to give knob D four turns to the left, and this takes him back to the starting position.
B 35. His formula is actually a very simple one: 2 (+3) = 5 (+4) = 9 (+5) = 14 (+6) = 20 (+7) = 27 (+8) = 35.

Page 133
See drawing.
The seal only
travels on
paths that
pass between
two areas in
which the
number in one area is exactly double the number in
the other.

2	7	5	2	10	6	4	5
6	2	8	4	5	3	2	4
6	2	4	10	3	6	1	7
2	1	10	5	10	3	6	2
3	2	5	7	5	6	5	1

Page 134
The system is based on a yellow - red - blue - green
sequence. The binder between 2 and 3, the one with
a yellow-blue sticker, has disappeared.

Page 135
He cannot have painted painting number one. because
he would have needed at least 7 colors, including black
and white.

Page 136
A2, B3, C4, D1. The parts between the grains of the leaves of a set allow you to constitute a complete green leaf and a complete brown leaf.

Page 137
A left downward arrow allows you to trace a path from arrow to arrow that uses all the keys on the keyboard, starting from any key.

Page 138
This is the pattern according to which the rounds are being moved about. Consequently the correct answer is disc 1.

Page 139
A L. The first letter has three dashes: E. The second letter has two dashes: F. The third letter has one dash: L. The fourth letter has no dash: I
B Group 2. None of the other groups includes the large surrounding form.

Page 140
Nail 4-2. The row column sum is six at each attachment.

Page 141
Key number 4. In the case of all the other keys, the number of notches and teeth is increased by one each time.

Page 142
Each time the burglar picks the middle floor of a building that has an odd number of floors. He will consequently break next into building number 5.

Page 143
Flower number 4. From the other situations it appears that the color order in descending order of dominance is: blue (most dominant), followed by white, red, orange, yellow, and finally (least dominant), purple.

Page 144
The second floor. The elevator stops on each floor that has the figure two.

Page 145
The refrain stretches from note 14 to note 20.

Page 146
1/5 and 6/7.

Page 147
On position 2. The top figure of each stack is the same as the bottom figure of the previous stack.

Page 148
11. All the keys on the corner points of a black, blue, red, and yellow square belong together.

Page 149
On page 48. If the colored field is orange, the next colored face will be found 5 pages further into the

book. If the colored face is green, the next colored face will be found 7 pages further on. The next colored field will consequently be found 7 pages further into the book.

Page 150
Shield number 6. In all the other cases, the white square is located above a red-blue plane.

Page 151
Point 6. Follow line 1 to point 2, line 2 to point 3, line 3 to point 4, line 4 to point 5, and line 5 to point 6.

Page 152
27282635. Each digit of the figure on the first ring is, each time, increased by the figure that indicates the place of the letter on the ring in the alphabet. A = 1209. D = 1(+4) = 5, 2 (+4) = 6, 0 (+4) = 4, 9 (+4) = 13. Z = 1 (+26) = 27, 2 (+26) = 28, 0 (+26) = 26, 9 (+26) = 35.

Page 153
Shape 4. The red plane should be dark blue.

Page 154
View number 2. The green line of the wheel axle cannot be at the front of the train.

Page 155
6. The tan, green, and blue blocks have have thread A. The white and orange blocks have thread B.

Page 156
Stained-glass window 2. Just count the colors and the formats in the broken windows and you will find the correct answer.

Page 157
7. In the upper row you will find all the figures that have been placed around the figure 1, in the second row all the figures around figure 7, and in the third row you will find all the figures around figure 2 in the second row.

Page 158
Yes. Pile up 27 identical cubes, then turn the middle cube until the correct color appears.

Page 159
Figure 1. In the case of an even number on the outer ring the inner ring points at 0, and in the case of an odd figure the ring points at 1.

Page 160
14352. The color of the star corresponds to the cap of the same color.

Page 161
Ballpoint pen 4. In the case of all the other ballpoint pens the second and fourth dots, starting from the top, have the same color.

Page 162
Place number 7. The back face must be mirrored.

Page 163
Brown block

Page 164
Work of art number 4. In all the other artworks,
the shapes that share the same colors can be found
in the same positions.

Page 165
On base number 8. Levels and walls all have their
own particular identical color.

Page 166
Roll number 2.

Page 167
7. Count the missing blocks in each opening.

Page 168
The order is 1 - 3 - 4 - 2 - 5. The 8-pixel snake
is moving one pixel each time.

Page 169
CD 2 should go in position B. The outer circle rotates 90° counterclockwise each time, the middle circle 90° clockwise, and the inner circle 180°.

Page 170
Colors 1, 4, 6, 7, and 8. (If you mix the colors, you can't get the colors you started with.)

Page 171
RH, CW, and AY. The sum of the places the letters occupy in the alphabet invariably equals 26.

Page 172
Like figure 4. Each laughing face has a sun with 7 beams. Left foot to the left/right = left hand pointing upward/downward. Right foot to the left/right = right hand pointing downward/upward.

Page 173
Three. See drawing.

Page 174
An eye looking to the right is missing on square 18.

Page 175
AJ, BG, CL, DK, EH, FI.

Page 176
LTI

Page 177
A Folding the ground plan will give you cube 1.
B Cube 2. Cubes 2 and 5 have the same right
*   lateral face, so one of them must be wrong.*
*   On closer inspection, you will find that*
*   cube 2 is not identical with the other four.*

Page 178
4. There is an even-numbered block at each
of the intersections.

Page 179
CYBERSPACE

Page 180
32. The figures 1 to 9 have been grouped by
three and are inserted between a multiple of four
(which increases by a factor of two): (4) 123
(8) 456 (16) 789 (32).

Page 181
A thin line. Starting from the middle, the left
part of the bar code is the mirror image of
the right part.

Page 182
You will be back in starting position after
signpost 8.

Page 183
Exchange row B for row I.

Page 184
VUD. Each letter moves up one place in the alphabet
at the other side of a horizontal or vertical line.

Page 185
In the case of the fourth group (the one with the arrows pointing left), the arrows are rotated 90 degrees. All the other arrows have been rotated 45 degrees.

Page 186
All the blocks are repeated following a diagonal that runs from the upper left corner to the lower right corner. Only block 3 does not do that.

Page 187
Line number 3 does not respect the following color sequence: green - white - yellow - purple - red - grey - dark purple - light blue - brown.

Page 188
A7. There are three groups of cubes: figures, letters, and colors. There are no rules within a group. Figures can be freely combined with figures, colors with

colors, etc. However between the groups the following rules apply: figure 1 can only be combined with letter A or with color red. 2 with B or yellow, 3 with C or blue and 4 with D or green. So A7= C.

Page 189
CABC. The sequence repeats itself after each third printing plate. What with the mistake that has been made, the sequence on plate 30 is CCAB. Sequence ABCA starts again after printing plate 31. It follows that we are left with 100 − 31 = 69 plates. As 69 can be divided by 3, the 100th printing plate will be the same as the third plate, i.e., CABC.

Page 190
At point 7. The graph follows the indications of the arrows on the vertical and horizontal axis. Whenever the line crosses a circle, the former movement is repeated, disregarding the indications given by the arrows.

Page 191
Picture number 4. For the picture to derive from the same cube, the pink faces should be yellow.

Page 192
Cube number three.

Page 193
Cube 3. The first cube is given successive 120 degrees frontal turns. After three turns the circle is closed (360°) and the cube is back in position A.

Page 194
26. The additional number each time equals the sum of the individual figures of the crossed numbers: 1+1+1+2+0+2+7+3+3+4+2 = 26.

Page 195
2 minutes. In each group of 4 CDs, the product of two of the CD times minus the third time equals the

time on the central CD. For the last group, this means
42 x 2) – 31 = 53.

Page 196
Beam 3.

Page 197
After compass 12 you will be back at the starting point.

Page 198
Share 481413. In all the other cases the sum of the
first and the last digits, the sum of the second and the
penultimate digits, and the sum of the two middle
figures are identical.

Page 199
Cube 1. All the other cubes have been laid out
following a red and blue moiré cross pattern.

Page 200
In the case of cube 6, the colored faces are not in the
right place.

Page 201
Picture 3. On the face of die number 3 with a value of 1, the white spot must be in the right upper corner for the picture to be identical with the other four.

Page 202
Ball number 7. These are the rules that apply to the set. The euro symbols all appear on purple balls, the dollar signs on green balls. the even numbers on yellow balls, the odd numbers and the consonants on orange balls, and all the vowels on blue balls. The numbers from 1–9 have been printed in red, 10–19 in white, and 20–29 in black. In order to belong to this set, number 7 on the orange ball ought to have been printed in red.

Page 203
On tile B. The walker changes directions on the first tile that has the same color as the tile at the end of the path that includes two equal colors and will take the direction of the two equally colored tiles.

Page 204
Tunnels: AF, BD, CN, EP, GI, HJ and MQ. Recesses: K, L, and O.

Great Color
Optical Illusions
Answers

Page 206
It's clear now that the eyes on Grandpa's face have
been duplicated. At first glance, however, our eyes find
it difficult to understand such a repetition, so they
automatically correct for it. When you first looked,
you probably thought you were looking at a normal
face.

Page 207
Either one because the design reverses.

Page 208
The valleys become peaks and the peaks change
into valleys.

Page 209
Turn the page upside down. It's the symbol of England
— the British Bulldog.

Page 210
A black rabbit in a white circle.

Page 211
The steam engine goes backwards.

Page 212
(top) A bird in the the hand.
(bottom) It works because all the words in the
orange panels have horizontal symmetry.

Page 213
Joseph Stalin.

Page 214
Look at the page from a distance and you'll see
Abraham Lincoln.

Page 215
The word CELERY is unreadable. You can read the
word TOMATO because the letters used all have
vertical symmetry.

Page 216
It looks like a man's head; a barrel maker is called a COOPER.

Page 217
Turn the page upside down to see his wife Judy. The word "punch" has been written in such a way that it is still readable when viewed upside down.

Page 218
Look in the triangle.

Page 219
The choice is yours!

Page 220
Vertical stripes make the ceiling look higher. Horizontal stripes make the room look bigger — so will a mirror.

Page 221
The mother-in-law.

Page 222
You see perfectly straight lines and squares.

Page 223
Slowly bring the page closer to your face.

Page 224
A Dalmatian dog in a snow scene.

Page 225
LIONEL — turn the page upside down.

Page 226
You can see them in the trees, but only if you turn the page upside down.

Page 227
The portrait is made up of different typefaces.

Page 228
Turn the page 90 degrees clockwise and you will see a dog curled up on a small carpet.

Page 229
This is called a Jordan Curve — it is a circle twisted out of shape. If you look at it carefully you will see that the red dot is inside the circle, because a line from it crosses the curve an odd number of times.

Page 230
A clown wearing a three-pointed hat.

Page 231
A red stop sign.

Page 232
Turn the page 90 degrees counterclockwise, Look
carefully at the shapes and you'll see the words "We
see but don't observe" and their mirror images.

Page 233
Turning the page 90 degrees clockwise changes the
picture into the giant's profile.

Page 234
Of course you can! Turn the page upside down to
make the weird rabbit appear.

Page 235
There are two side profile faces looking at each other.
When combined, they form a third face that is looking
straight ahead.

Page 236
Look at the illustration again. A large head fills
the lower right-hand corner, another cow behind
faces left.

Page 237
It's a very early example of "morphing" — the dog
changes into the man and it goes on and on, in an ever
increasing way.

Page 238
(top) Is it an old-fashioned telephone or a picture
of two dogs looking at each other? It's both. It all
depends on how you look at it.(bottom) They are
both the same size, but the curves make number
1 look bigger.

Page 239
Turn the page upside down — their faces are formed
by the plates the juggler is balancing.

Page 240
The dentist extracts the tooth.

Page 241
A beggar holding out a hand — or the profile of a goofy face.

Page 242
Look at the reflection of this page in a mirror.
It changes to say SPIT IN THE SPITTOON.

Page 243
It only looks like a spiral. It's actually a series of concentric circles. To prove they are circles, trace one of them out with a compass.

Page 244
It all depends on how you look at it.

Page 245
The smoke is blowing to one side and the flag is blowing the other way.

Page 246
You will see a pink heart.

Page 247
They appear to hold hands.

Page 248
The upside down page reveals an animal side.

Page 249
Give the page a quarter turn to the left.

Page 250
The word is KEITH.

Page 251
Turn the page upside down to see Finlay Dunn's extra faces.

Page 252
Look carefully. The word SUMMER has been repeated to give the abstract shape.

Page 253
Viewed close up, a young lady looks at her reflection. At a distance, it's a grinning skull.

Page 254
The missing word is LAST — turn the page upside down.

Page 255
Turn the picture upside down to see it.

Page 256
They are both the same size, but when one is turned to look like a diamond, it looks bigger.

Page 257
Another of those Victorian grinning skulls.

Page 258
Invert the page to see Churchill's head under the arm of the sailor turning the wheel.

Page 259
It's up to you.

Page 260
Turn the page a quarter turn to the left.

Page 261
The clock was upside down.

Page 262
Look at her face. It's made up from a picture of her son wearing a hat and with sack on his shoulder.

Page 263
They are both the same length.

Page 264
It shows some of the characters Lord Byron (who was a poet) wrote about.

Page 265
See illustration.

Page 266
The banana tree shows the fruit growing down instead of up.

Page 267
You will see 3 hats and 2 stars.

Page 268
Another picture in which the choice is yours.

Page 269
A boy blowing a bugle. See illustration.

Page 270
They join up perfectly.

Page 271
Cover the faces so that just their eyes are visible
and you will see that they are identical.

Page 272
It's your decision.

Page 273
A polar bear in a snowstorm.

Page 274
The letter E.

Page 275
To make sense of what we see, our brain leaps ahead,
closing the top of the second H to an A.

Page 276
The ball disappears.

Page 277
The clergyman prays for peace, the Kaiser preys on the people.

Page 278
It's a "magic square" — in this case each horizontal, vertical, and diagonal line adds up to 24. It also works if you turn it upside down.

Page 279
An accented conversation in a restaurant.
    Have you any eggs?
    Yes, we have eggs.
    Have you any ham?
    Yes, we have ham.
    OK, we have ham and eggs for 2.

Page 280
78. It's up to you.

Page 281
Take your pick.

Page 282
First count the flames — 5. Now count the base of
each candle, and you'll find that there are 7.

Page 283
Turn the page so that the arrow points to the left —
you should be able to read the words.